MW00987453

Witch on the Go

Witch on the Go

A Book of Spells to Take with You

Cal Garrison

Red Wheel
Boston, MA / York Beach, ME

First published in 2005 by
Red Wheel/Weiser, LLC
York Beach, ME
With offices at:
368 Congress Street
Boston, MA 02210
www.redwheelweiser.com

Library of Congress Cataloging-in-Publication Data

Garrison, Cal.
    Witch on the go : a book of spells to take with you / Cal Garrison.
        p. cm.
    ISBN 1-59003-071-0 (alk. paper)
    1. Witchcraft. 2.   Charms. 3.   Magic.   I. Title.
    BF1571.G37 2005
    133.4'4–dc22

                        2004020010

Typeset in Kennerly 10/13 by Garrett Brown
Printed in Canada
TCP

12 11 10 09 08 07 06 05
  8 7 6 5 4 3 2 1

Contents

Introduction

don't know how qualified I am to write this book. It took me forever to get my show on the road. To be honest with you, being "on the go" has never been my thing. My mother still goes on about how my birth was induced with a bottle of castor oil because I was three weeks late and the rest of the family needed to move to New Hampshire.

My reluctance to incarnate on the Earth Plane was punctuated by the fact that when I finally came out I was born sideways. I didn't learn to walk until I was eighteen months old, and I didn't own a car until I was thirty-five. Up until then I used a bicycle and walked a *lot*. I took the bus. I bummed rides. And hitchhiking was resorted to on occasion.

The simple act of getting from A to B has always been a little different in my world. And as far as ambition is concerned, forget about it! I prefer to float around in the aether, and I don't even have a *one-day* plan, let alone a five-year one. Back in 2001 the universe forced me to abandon my laid-back ways the night my editor, Jan Johnson, called me up and asked me to write my first book. Waking up to the whole concept of being on the go was more or less induced at that point, the same way my birth was.

In thinking about how to write this book, I realized that being on the go has something to do with going out and "getting a life." And if that's something you've already handled, then being on the go simply means that you have a life. When a woman has a life, she's connected to herself and, by extension, to many other things. And all these things she's connected to require her to be moving around a lot.

Keeping it together is a full-time job. Not only do you have a million external things to be responsible for, all the inner stuff needs to be maintained too. If you don't do your spiritual work, you get mired in the outer stuff and completely lose your way. Any card-carrying witch *needs* peace and quiet because magic is an art, and witchcraft takes time. Peace and quiet are hard to come by when your schedule is full.

If you're a witch and happen to be on the go as well, spending half a day or longer out in the woods conjuring things up is out of the question. When I was younger and freer it was totally within my time budget to dance around a fire and grind herbs in my mortar and pestle for hours on end. And there is something absolutely incredible about being able to do this. It's hard to beat. Back in the old days, I could even get together with good friends and share the experience.

Now that I'm post-menopausal and graced with the wisdom that comes with cronehood, it seems as if I have more responsibility for what I know about being a witch. And the way things are at this point, on the day of any major cross quarter I'm either on my way to a book signing or sitting on a plane heading off toward one of the Four Directions. For those of you who are unfamiliar with the term "cross quarter" this refers to a major turning point in the yearly cycle. There are eight of these Wiccan holidays. On these dates the veil that separates the world of spirit from the world of the living is so thin that it makes all your spell work more potent.

It may have taken me eighteen months to learn to walk, but since 2001 my life has been a "space odyssey," literally. Going at warp speed is just as much fun as mixing potions at the kitchen table, but it has its drawbacks. When your life is full you don't have time to honor the Great Mother in the traditional way any more. At first this bothered me. It seemed so ironic that I had turned into sort of a spokesperson for the Craft, yet I couldn't even fit a spell or two into my schedule–until I figured out that magic is everywhere, all the time, and in *everything* we do.

While I am rarely able to do it up and go full tilt the way I used to, I have found ways to do magic wherever I am, with whatever I have, and it works just fine. In a lot of ways it's more creative because you have to be very observant, inventive, and clear.

One of the things that being a witch on the go has really taught me is that, when you're doing spell work, it truly *is* your intention and what you hold in your mind that matters the most. You don't necessarily need to go through a lot of rigmarole. You don't *need* "sacred space," because all space is sacred. You don't need an altar, and an Athame, otherwise known as a ritual blade, isn't necessary either. Your lap is the ultimate altar, and a Swiss Army knife, or even a plastic one, works fine. You don't even need salt to cast a circle if you don't have any on hand. And you can call in the Guardians any time you want because these archetypal beings who watch over the Four Directions live in your mind and heart as well as in the spiritual realms. They are always there, wherever you are.

Traditional witches may have a problem with everything I'm saying–but, hey, let's get real! If your life is such that you have the freedom to honor every cross quarter and lunar phase in the grand manner, more power to you! This book is being written for those of you who are just as busy as I am but who don't want to lose touch with the magic in their lives.

The spells that follow will give you something to go by, but the whole point here is to free you up to find your own unique approach. There's no excuse to pass up doing spell work just because you're on the highway, at the airport, or too busy handing out candy to the trick-ortreaters on Halloween. Be creative, give yourself permission to dispense with ritual, and trust the fact that what you do while you're on the go will be just as effective as what you would be able to do if you had more time. You will find that magic "outside of the box" works like a charm.

Have fun with these spells! I hope they serve to introduce you to a whole new way of relating to magic, and help you to maintain your connection to your inner work in the midst of all the other wonderful things you got put here to do.

Chapter 1

Simple Basics

When I'm at home in Vermont, I never have to worry about whether I have what I need to do circle work or cast a spell. The whole house is filled with witchy things. If Martha Stewart came to call, she'd think someone had spiked her hand-squeezed lemonade! (Actually, if Martha Stewart were more enlightened, she'd realize that underneath it all she's probably a witch at heart.)

I keep a big basket full of herbs, stones, bones, and ribbons right at the foot of my bed. And in the kitchen I have a special cupboard stocked with oils, roots, and more exotic items like incense, fingernails, and hair. There are bottles and candles and goblets all over the place, and they're not for decoration. I *use* them. Every good witch has these things, and over time they accumulate conveniently so that you don't ever have to go looking for what you need when the full Moon rolls around.

Because I'm on the road a lot, and busy doing different things, I don't always have access to my cache of witchy paraphernalia. Sometimes I'm away from home for a month at a time. And in between, like any other woman who has a life, I'm too busy to do formal rituals. Very often, the full Moon catches me by surprise, and on Midsummer Night, I may not happen to be casting spells in my kitchen, because I'm doing a horoscope or out with one of my boyfriends.

In the old days I was religious about setting aside certain dates to focus exclusively on witchcraft. Don't ask me what happened, but I am just not as obsessed with marking time in the traditional way any more. Something in me has realized that you just don't have to get that uptight about it, and at a certain level, if you're too rigidly correct about these things, it can take all the fun out of life. I also recognize that we are connected to cosmic forces all the time, wherever we are, and no matter what we're doing.

But the witch in me loves magic. And sometimes when I'm out and about and it happens to be a major cross quarter, I wish that I had something handy to work a spell with. If you're really tuned into things, it's easy to make magic with virtually nothing, but there are certain items it helps to have around.

The Portable Spell Kit

One day I woke up and realized that I could carry an all-purpose, portable spell kit in my purse and bring it along wherever I go, so that if for any reason I wanted or needed to do a spell or formally honor a cross quarter, I wouldn't have to run all over the place looking for a magic shop. In case you haven't noticed, the Christian Coalition has a lot more clout in this country than the League of Witches does. There *are* no magic shops in Greeley, Colorado, and they don't have one in Plattsburg, New York, either! If it's Beltane and you're out in the boon-

docks looking for mistletoe on the eve of this important fertility celebration, you might as well be on a quest for the Holy Grail!

What follows is a list of magical items that I keep with me all the
time. This is something I came up with out of necessity, and any witch
who's on the go will love the idea—if she hasn't already thought of it
herself.

The Portable Spell Kit

What you will need:

An empty Altoids tin
A one-dram bottle of musk oil
A small quartz crystal
A book of matches
A few multicolored birthday candles
Some Post-it notes
Some black thread
Some red thread

Life is pretty simple when you get right down to it, isn't it? With all the
crazy things I used to do magic with, it amazed me when I realized that
what's listed above will cover just about anything.

I use an Altoids tin because it's inconspicuous. When the security
forces at the airport are rifling through my purse, they assume that I
have mints in there and don't bother opening it up. But if they do, it's
easy to blow it off. One time the guys at Denver International took a
peek into my little tin. They gave me a look and I gave them a laugh
when I told them I was a MacGyver groupie!

Those of you who aren't constantly having the contents of your
purse inspected could use a bigger container. This would allow you to

add more items and create a fancier kit. For instance, instead of birthday candles, you could carry mini-candles, which are better because they burn longer.

If you do most of your moving around in a car, you can keep *all* of your magic stuff right in the trunk. One of the reasons I work with an Altoids tin is that it fits in my pocket. If I'm at one of those highway rest stops and have to walk out into the woods a ways to work a spell, it looks less suspicious to have everything on my person. Normally the people in those places leave you alone because they think you're just out in the bushes taking a leak. But if you're walking around with a bumpy looking satchel, out in the middle of nowhere, some concerned citizen is going to think that you're a terrorist or a suicidal runaway. And they will either feel called to do their civic duty and report you, or to come out and deliver a sermon on the pros and cons of living. People are nosy—all of us are. The good thing about this portable spell kit is that you can bring it anywhere without attracting unwanted attention.

As far as lighting candles goes, all I can say is, use your best judgment. If you're outside and the fire wardens have put a ban on burning, don't even think of including candles in your magic. And if you're at the airport or in the subway station, forget about the fire element! You don't want to wind up in jail.

At the office it *may* be a different story. After all, there are candles on every office birthday party cake. And if no one's around, sometimes you can get away with it. But don't light candles in the ladies' room. Someone might interrupt you, and there are so many rules about smoking that you'd get snitched on for having a cigarette. If you're in a motel room, candles are fine, but it'll be less of a hassle if you ask for a smoking room when you make your reservations. People are weird about smoke and fire, so as far as this aspect of your on-the-go spell work is concerned, just be smart about it or it'll draw too much attention to what you're

8

doing. And, of course, never leave a burning candle unattended!

I use musk oil in my portable kit because it's totally all-purpose. Musk works for love, money, success, and banishing. As far as oils go, you just can't beat it. It also functions to strengthen any spell you might want to do at a deeper level for your own spiritual growth. You could use patchouli oil instead, if you prefer it. Patchouli is another one of those oils that goes well with any type of spell.

Whether I'm at home or on the road, I always anoint my candles, so this is one use for the oil. I also use oils to anoint my "third eye" prior to doing any kind of magic. That space between your eyebrows is a portal to the higher self, and the oil amplifies the connection to the part of your brain that knows exactly what it's doing.

Anyone who does spell work has to deal with endless chatter from the pain in the butt that hangs out in her head and says things like, "You're crazy, this isn't going to work" or, "Who do you think you are?" This stuff comes up constantly, but with practice you learn to just ignore it. Charging the third eye functions to tune you in to the aspect of your consciousness that knows better than to be intimidated by what your mind thinks.

I dab a few drops of oil on whatever I write, too. That's what the Post-it notes are for. When you do a spell, it's good to make up a rhyme that captures the essence of what you're wishing for. Don't worry—you don't have to be a Pulitzer Prize winner to do this. As long as your heart's in it, any old rhyme will do.

And if you have a mental block about your poetic ability, you can express your intentions in plain English, or use symbols if it's easier. Even though Post-it notes are tiny, if you condense your thoughts and write small enough, you can pack a lot of words onto those little slips of paper. If you're outdoors and you've run out of Post-its, you can use leaves or birch bark instead of paper.

The thread is good to have because, after you've written whatever you're going to write, you can fold the paper and tie it up to "bind" the spell, or symbolically "wrap things up," so to speak. Besides, you see, once you're done with a spell, you'll have this folded slip of paper floating around in your purse. If you keep it untied anyone could find it, open it up, and read it. People are less inclined to snoop when things are tied up. They may think you're obsessive-compulsive or slightly insane, but they won't bother to read it.

If you were working in the privacy of your own home you would burn your spells, and all the information on the paper would go up in smoke and merge with the Unified Field, that matrix upon which physical reality is woven. But lighting things on fire when you're at the office could get *you* fired. Burning little pieces of paper in public places just isn't a good idea. That's why I keep thread around.

Pens are pretty easy to come by, so I didn't bother to include them in my kit list. I *have* been in situations where I couldn't get my hands on a pen, so if you want to play it safe pop one of those little pencils that come with every board game into your kit.

The quartz crystal is there for insurance. When you're on the road or at the office, time is always of the essence, and when you're in a hurry it's hard to focus. This is the only drawback to on-the-go spells. Sometimes you just don't feel that you have enough time to drive the point home.

The nice thing about quartz crystals is they have the capacity to store information like little tiny computers. They're very receptive to thoughts, and you can program them quite easily with your mind. So whatever you are trying to accomplish with any spell can be formulated clearly with a few words, and the thought form, or intention, behind it can be put into and held inside the crystal. This is why I say crystals offer a form of spell insurance. They actually hold all the thoughts that you may feel too rushed to concentrate on.

Before you charge the crystal, you'll need to clear it. Crystals are so receptive to thoughts and other forms of energy they absorb everything in the atmosphere around them. The ones you buy at the store, for instance, are full of the vibrations of every customer who came along and touched them. These extraneous energies need to be cleared or removed or there will be no room in the crystal for *your* intentions. There are a million ways to do this. The quickest way is to blow on it. You can also step into any rest room and rinse it in the sink. If you're outside near a stream or at the beach, stick your crystal in the water for a few minutes and you'll be all set. Once the quartz is cleared, you can program it with your intentions.

All crystals have six terminations, or facets, that meet at the point. Each termination can hold one "program." I never overload a crystal with more than one program, but it *can* be done. The average person has one major issue that is "spell-worthy" at any given time. And it's best to handle one thing at a time, for a couple of reasons. Everything is connected, so if you effect changes in one set of conditions, the result will spill over and alter every other aspect of your life as well. And you sort of have to wait and see how the chips fall before doing another spell.

For instance, if you program a crystal to attract a lover, and a millionaire shows up, this circumvents the need to charge the same crystal to attract money. The other thing is that we all get neurotic sometimes, and this keeps us out of touch with what's important. Even though you may feel as if *everything* is screwed up, ultimately life is much simpler than we allow it to be.

If you're in a chaotic space, charging a crystal with six different intentions suggests that there's too much fear fueling the work at hand. It's unfair to expect a crystal to handle what you can't, so get centered and clear about whatever the *main* issue is before you do any crystal programming. When you know exactly what you want to manifest, hold one of the terminations up to your third eye and send those thoughts right into the crystal. Carry it in your pocket or on your body for as long as it takes the spell to work. The quartz will hold those intentions for you until they come into being, or until you clear the crystal again. You will be quite surprised at how effective these beautiful little earthstars are.

Circles, Salt, and Other Things

I haven't said anything about casting circles when you're on the go, and this issue needs to be addressed. Every spell works better if it's done inside a circle. It's inappropriate to sprinkle salt around the office. You can't do it at the airport either. In these situations your best bet is to cast a circle energetically. Just put it out there with your mind.

If you're working outside, you can cast an energetic circle or draw one in the dirt with a stick. At the beach all you have to do is draw a circle in the sand. And there are always rocks and twigs and leaves out in wooded areas that are excellent for creating circles with.

If you do have salt, use it. It takes approximately one hundred packets of salt from McDonald's or Wendy's or Burger King to cast a circle. Whoever's in line behind you might make a few comments about your blood pressure, but this is what you're up against if you're one of those people who absolutely *has* to work with salt. As a more realistic alternative, you can carry one of those cardboard Morton's saltshakers in your car or purse at all times. If you're desperate, run into a convenience store or a grocery and get a cheap cardboard salt and pepper set.

You can connect with the Four Directions mentally too. You'd be surprised how easy it is to do this. Once I "see" the circle in my inner vision, I sit quietly and send my thoughts to each of the Four Directions and call the Guardians in silently with the same words I would use if I were speaking out loud.

The Four Directions are the four cardinal points of the compass, which correspond to the four elements: North (Earth), East (Air), South (Fire), and West (Water). They form the cross of matter, or the axis upon which physical reality is suspended. The Guardians that watch over each direction need to be invoked, or called in, every time you cast a circle. Their presence supports the spell and protects you from any negative energies that might interfere with its outcome. In a formal ritual you would call in the Guardians out loud. When you're on the go, it's more appropriate to call them in silently, with the same reverence you would have if you were doing this in the privacy of your own space. I have included instructions for calling in the Guardians in an appendix at the end of this book. You can follow them or make up your own method.

As far as an Athame goes, I use a Swiss Army knife. A Swiss Army knife is good to have around for a million other reasons too. It's not a cool thing to bring to the airport, however, because the security people confiscate things like this and send you off to reckon with stricter, more unpleasant individuals. If you're hellbent on using an Athame at the airport, a plastic knife from one of the kiosks is your best bet.

Herbs, Weeds, and Other Good Things to Know About

What about herbs? This is one of my favorite subjects. We all use herbs in our spells, and there's no need to exclude them from your magic while you're on the go. Herbs amplify everything you do. After you anoint your candles, if you roll them in the appropriate herbal mixture it gives your spell an extra kick. Wrapping the right herbs inside your Post-it notes is also a good idea. The thing is, you never know what you're going to need, and it's a hassle carrying weeds and powders everywhere you go.

I have been doing this for a long time and one of the things that

I've figured out is that you can find exactly the right herb wherever you happen to be. What follows is a list of easily recognizable things that grow everywhere or can be found anywhere, and chances are that you can recognize them on sight.

Included in the following list is a description of what spells these particular herbs, fruits, and weeds can be used for. This information covers *any* type of wish a person could possibly have. All you have to do is memorize it—otherwise you'll be stuck having to bring this book along wherever you go.

On-the-Go Herbal

Apples–Apples are the most magical fruit. They're used in love spells primarily, but they're also good for attracting money. The Tree of Life was an apple tree, so this fruit can be used in spells that have to do with promoting longevity or gaining knowledge. Just eating an apple can turn into a love spell if you do it with intent. You can also carve your intentions right into the skin and bury the apple, toss it into any body of moving water, or walk up to the top of a hill and cast it to one of the Four Directions.

Beets–Beets are used in love magic. If you carve your wish right into the root with your Swiss Army knife and bury it wherever you are, you've got yourself a spell! Beet juice makes good ink, especially for writing love spells. You can dip a twig in the juice and write with that, but it's easier to carve a pen right out of the beet itself.

Burdock–These are the burrs that get stuck to your clothing when you're out walking in the fields. They love animal fur too! *Any* part of the burdock plant can be used. This weed grows everywhere, and it's a protection herb. Burdock leaves worn inside your shoes protect against illness. If you're on the road and coming down with the flu, find a couple of burdock leaves and stick them inside your shoes.

Cedar–Cedar trees come in different varieties and they are everywhere. The bark, the boughs, and the berries are all usable. Cedar chips are *really* plentiful. They're used as a mulch and you can find them at any mall, believe it or not, in the gardening department. They're also right outside most public buildings or wherever there's a lot of landscaping. The reason cedar is used in closets and saunas is that it "gets the bugs out," so any part of the tree can be used to purify, protect, and cleanse situations. It's good for attracting money, too. Or love. If you want to sharpen your psychic abilities, cedar is what you need.

Clover–Clover leaves and flowers are good for attracting money, luck, and love. They also act to protect you. A clover leaf in your shoe will protect you from any sort of evil or negativity.

Coffee–Coffee is used in spells where there is a need to hasten or speed things up. You can get it to go or brew it yourself. Just sipping a cup of coffee can be a magical act. You can combine it with other elements and issues. If you want to materialize money quickly, stick a sprig of clover in your coffee and drink every drop with intent. You could do the same thing and focus on love, if that's your wish.

Dandelion flowers, leaves, or roots–Any part of a dandelion is good for spells that have to do with improving your health or strengthening you physically. Dandelion spells are also good if it's your intention to lose weight.

Grass–Yes, believe it or not, grass is magical! It binds every wish and makes it come true. If you're in a grassy area you can tie knots in the grass and build a wonderful circle that way. And one of the simplest spells is to hold a blade of green grass up to your lips and speak your wish into it. Then take the grass and rub it on a pebble or a small stone until it leaves a green mark. Carry the stone with you until the wish comes true, then bury it in the ground or toss it into any body of moving water.

Juniper–Juniper is one of those shrubs that every landscaper uses as a bedding plant. It's so commonplace that if you weren't a witch you wouldn't even notice it. You can find it out in the fields, too. Anything that cedar can do, juniper can do. The blue berries on this plant are used in spells when you want to make yourself beautiful. They are also used for weight loss. I carry juniper berries in my pocket whenever I want to look like a million bucks.

Maple–Maple trees grow everywhere. You can use the leaves and bark for both love and money spells. Maple branches make great wands, and maple leaves can be used to write spells on, if you're out of paper.

Oak–Oak trees live a long time. Magically, any part of an oak tree is useful for long life, fertility, male potency, and all-around good luck. Oak leaves are also good to use in place of paper if you've run out of Post-it notes. Acorns are magical too. If you bury an acorn when the Moon is waning, it will bring money into your life.

Palm–Palm leaves are for peace, love, and hope. The leaves of the date palm are also used for fertility and virility. If you're being stalked or troubled by someone who seems a little too weird and won't go away, carry a palm leaf with you or place one outside the door of your motel room. But if you feel threatened, notify the authorities, to be on the safe side!

Peaches–Peaches are used magically to attract love. Slice it, dice it, or eat it whole, you can win anyone's heart with a peach. A peach can be used if fertility is what you're after, too. They have also long been used to drive evil away. The seeds are best for this. Carry one in your pocket if you're all alone in the big city. It won't replace a .38 Special or a can of pepper spray if you really get into a jam, but it will remind you that your spirit guides are always there and lessen feelings of paranoia that often attract danger.

Pears–Pears are for love and sex magic. If you're in the mood, or you want someone else to be, use a pear to turn up the heat.

Pepper–Pepper is for lust and wild lovemaking. If you're on the go *and* on the make, stock up on those little packets of black pepper they provide at every fast-food chain!

Pine–Pine needles are used in success spells or in any situation where you want to make a good impression. They are also good when you're in need of protection or surrounded by evil influences. If someone's giving you a hard time, you can use any part of a pine tree to send their negativity right back to them.

Potatoes–Potatoes are mainly used for health. Some people say they can be used in spells to make warts disappear. Some say that if you carry a potato in your purse all winter, you will never get sick.

Plantain–Plantain grows close to the ground, and the leaves spread out flat around the stem. This is one of those weeds no one even notices. It grounds, solidifies, and protects your finances. Plantain is also a protection herb. If you're in an area where there are a lot of snakes—and this includes the two-legged variety—stick a plantain leaf in your shoe.

Radishes—Radishes are used for love and lust. You can do anything you want with them, but just sleeping with a radish under your pillow is enough to attract these influences into your life.

Roses—You'll find rosebushes everywhere. They grow outside in the landscaped areas around any mall or public building. You can even pick them up at the Quickee Mart. Roses are used in love spells. They're also for fidelity. If for any reason faithfulness is an issue while you're on the road, a rose will help. If you're in a situation where there's an overload of stress, rose petals will calm things down. Rose hips are just as good for love spells as the flower itself, but the fruit of the rose can be used in healing spells too. Some people say that rose hips will bring your heart's desire to life.

Sesame seeds—Sesame seeds are good whenever you're doing a money spell. They are also useful whenever you're in a situation where there are unknown factors, unanswered questions, or unsolved mysteries. I am including them in this on-the-go herbal because you can find them at any fast-food place wherever you happen to be. And if you don't want to eat your Big Mac, you can always leave it for the crows, bears, or raccoons to feast on. They'll love you for it!

Skunk cabbage—Skunk Cabbage doesn't grow everywhere, and it's seasonal. You'll find it growing in the shade near rivers and streams in the spring. The leaves are fat and broad, and it's easy to recognize because it stinks! This herb is good for any type of legal issue. It's a good idea to carry dried skunk cabbage leaves in the glove compartment of your car. That way if you get stopped for speeding, you have quick access to the perfect herb for getting you off the hook. While you're waiting for the cop to get out of his cruiser, hold a skunk cabbage leaf in your left hand, and you'll see yourself getting a warning instead of a ticket.

Tea–Black tea is good for attracting wealth, strength, and courage. It's also used in spells that involve lust and sexual attraction. Fixing a cup of tea and drinking it can turn into an act of magic if you hold your mind and heart focused on what you want. Adding an herb or two is a good idea if you feel like making things more specific.

Tobacco–Cigarettes are actually good for something, and you don't have to buy a whole pack. You can bum one off any smoker if you need tobacco for a spell. Whenever you want to connect with the spirit world, think of using tobacco. It's also useful when you feel as if you need protection. Whether you're traveling by water or land, sprinkle some tobacco in the water or out the car window, and it'll call in the Guardians who watch over you while you travel.

Tomatoes–Tomatoes were once referred to as "love apples." Just eating a tomato is good for drawing love to you, if that's your intent. They are also used to attract wealth.

Tumbleweed–Guess what this is good for? Traveling. Makes a lot of sense doesn't it? Tumbleweed is also really good in spells where the main focus is to find a sense of direction. This can be your life's direction, or a situation in which you're confused about where to move or where to go.

Alternative Courses of Action

I have to say that if you're in a city or an urban location, it's hard to find any of the herbs, leaves, and weeds listed above. I have found ways to get around this. You can check out the potted plants in any hotel or motel. Most of the time there's at least *one* plant that you can pinch a leaf or a bud from.

You can stop at any flower shop too, or pop into the health food store. Health food stores sell bulk herbs. If you want to make it easy on yourself, you can just buy a box of herbal tea, use what you need, and save the rest of the tea bags for drinking.

There are also nurseries and garden shops all over the place. If you really need herbs, go into the greenhouse at any nursery and you'll be delighted to find a bonanza of magical plants and flowers. Most of the time you don't even have to buy anything. There are dried buds on every single plant, and you're doing the nursery people a favor by picking them off and sticking them in your purse. Don't worry if someone gives you a weird look. If you want, just tell them you're a witch and they'll leave you alone!

What's listed above is bottom-line basic stuff. If you become totally familiar with what all these things are used for, that knowledge will help amplify your on-the-go magic.

It'll be your job from here on to be observant and pay attention to your surroundings so that you can utilize this information. Most people live in their heads so much that they have forgotten how to see what's right there in front of them. Part of being a good witch involves learning to notice everything. No matter where you are, absolutely everything in the immediate environment is imbued with its own magic and can be used for whatever you need, if you know what to do with it.

The Moon

There are a few other things we need to talk about. If you aren't naturally attuned to and aware of the lunar rhythms, you'd better get yourself one of those pocket Moon calendars and keep it with you all the time.

Ultimately it doesn't matter what day you do a spell on, if your intention is clear and strong enough. When you're on the road and feel the urge to do magic, just go for it. But if you're gone for any period of time and you have a *choice* about when you can do your spell work, pay attention to where the Moon is, and at least have a sense of whether it's waxing or waning. The waxing Moon will attract things into your life and expand or build up your wishes. It has an overall positive, plus effect. The waning cycle is for banishing things, dispelling negativity, and dealing with darker issues that you want to rid yourself of. Magic done under the appropriate lunar influence is more powerful, so keep that in mind and honor these two-week cycles as best you can.

Days of the Week

The days of the week vibrate differently too, and Monday's influence is different from Tuesday's. If it's possible to pick the appropriate day of the week to do your spells on, you should make an effort to do this. Here's a quick rundown on which day is good for what.

Monday—   Home, children, family, emotional issues, fertility, birthing, female stuff

Tuesday–	Sex, men, conflicts, strength, taking action, courage, ambition, accomplishing things, physical energy, sticking up for yourself
Wednesday–	Travel, writing, signing documents, schooling, communication, making things happen quickly
Thursday–	Court issues, attracting money, taking risks, bringing good luck to any situation, amplifying things, restoring faith and good will
Friday–	Love and money, beauty, artistic endeavors, self-worth issues–especially *love*
Saturday–	Banishing, cutting things off, ending things, binding influences
Sunday–	Success, health, wealth, spirituality, unity and oneness

North, South, East, and West

We're just about all set now. I have one more tip, however. You can always tell where the Four Directions are by watching the path the sun makes. It rises in the east and sets in the west, wherever you are. But on cloudy days, if you're in a strange place or stuck in a motel room or at a conference center, it's hard to know which way is up. In situations like this it's good to have a compass in your purse. I carry one with me all the time.

Aside from making sure you keep your glove compartment stocked with incense sticks and a small pocket mirror, that's about it. There's more I could say, but the point here is to keep it simple. Be loose, creative, and playful with this because the child in you is wiser than the adult you've become.

And don't limit yourself to what I have said. Remember, the word "witch" means *one who knows*. It's all about *wisdom*. The more knowledge you have about what you're doing, the more freedom you will have to really make good magic and have it work for you.

Chapter 2

Everyday Magical Acts

No matter what we do, there are certain things that happen every day for everyone. I don't care if you're a billionaire, a well-kept suburban housewife, a career woman, a factory girl, or a welfare mother, we all open our eyes in the morning and put our pants (skirts) on one leg at a time. And regardless of her circumstances, every woman I know hits the ground running and keeps running from morning till night.

The need to be on the go is a condition that appears to have been induced by the rigors of the fast-paced society we live in. But historically, women, perhaps even more than men, have always had too much to do. The saying "Man must work from sun to sun, but woman's work is never done" has been around for a long time. This condition makes it hard to find a few minutes to put on a little makeup, let alone sit for five hours out in the woods waving your wand and mixing potions.

Most women will tell you that they like the idea of being connected to the magic in their lives but that they never have a moment's peace. This issue has come up for me big time in the last three years, and I have tried really hard to reconcile my conflicting needs. Because magic is just as important to me as "having a life," I have had to figure out a way to get around this business of being too preoccupied to focus.

What I've learned through my involvement in spiritual work is that all of us are connected to Spirit in every moment and with every breath we take. That being the case, I have realized that I can make every thing I do, even the most mundane chores, into a spell if I want to. This has liberated me completely and made my magic much more spontaneous and fun. Now whenever I hear the song, "Every Little Thing She Does Is Magic," I chuckle inside because I know it's true.

What follows is a collection of things that anyone can do in the course of any day, no matter how busy or rushed she feels. I didn't read about this in a book; I made it all up because I had to. It was a matter of survival in a life that no longer provided me with the time I needed to be who I am.

So we're going to start with the moment we open our eyes, then move through the day to the point where we close them, with spells for each point along the way–"spells" that don't require any sort of ritual or rigmarole. These are more like magical acts that offer very powerful ways to make every single day more alive and meaningful. You can do any one, or all of them if you want to. It's totally up to you.

Morning

Every morning we open our eyes, leave our dreams, and enter the real world. I'm not so sure that life as we know it in the physical world is in fact the *real* world, but that's how most people see it. I live alone, and most of the time when I wake up I'm the only one in the bed. Whether you have company or not, you can still connect with yourself quietly without making a big deal out of it.

Invoking the Guardians

My way of doing this involves stretching out my arms to the right and to the left and stretching out my legs so that my body forms a cross. The way my bed is set up, I sleep with my head to the north. My feet point south, my right arm points west, and my left arm points east. As I do this I mentally honor the Four Directions and invoke the Guardians to come and watch over me during the day.

First I honor the Guardian of the Watchtower of the north by bringing my attention to the north point and mentally conjuring up the "being" who watches over that point in space. Everyone's perception of what this "being" looks like will be her own. The Guardians can take *any* form.

The spirit who guards me from the north point is a Native American chief with coal-black hair, dressed in his ceremonial clothes. He's very wise and loves me like a father.

When I bring my attention to my left arm, I am greeted by the Guardian who watches over my east point. This being is a Native American warrior. He's dressed in a loincloth and wears a wolf's head mask. He protects me and tells me how and when to stick up for myself.

I go next to my feet and invoke the Guardian of the Watchtower of the south. This being is a kachina, a Hopi ancestral spirit. She gives me spiritual information and support. She's the one who provides me with the ability to be receptive to miracles.

Then I go to my right arm to honor the western spirit. The being who guards my west point is an old Indian grandmother who sits and grinds corn in a stone bowl. She is full of wisdom, and her words are loaded with the kind of understanding only age can bring.

Before I even get up I bring all of these forces in, and each one will have something to say. Sometimes all they do is give me a look that tells me what I need to know. If there is anything specific that I need to focus on in the upcoming day, I ask the spirits who watch over the Four Directions to give me the strength to meet my responsibilities and approach everything I do with a joyful attitude.

Your Guardians will look different from mine, but anyone can connect with them. All you have to do is bring your attention to each point and wait for them to appear in your inner vision. Whatever, or whoever, shows up, *that's* your Guardian. I have never been deeply involved in Native American ways. My spiritual leanings are Wiccan, Celtic, and more based in the Norse belief systems. So it was quite a surprise to me that all of my Guardians were Native American archetypes, but that's what came in and they've been with me for a long time.

This process takes no effort at all. And aside from being completely receptive, the only thing you have to get straight is which way your body parts are pointing. When I've heard from all my Guardians and feel ready to go into the day, I thank each one, send them back to the four corners of the universe, get out of bed, and go about my business.

Morning Sex

Another way to get your energy flowing is to have sex in the morning. If you happen to have company when you wake up, you might as well take advantage of the opportunity to have every cell in your body light up! You don't necessarily need to make this a duet, though, and it's just as effective if you handle it yourself.

I don't know what's up with people, but they either take sex for granted or they have no clue about how potent it really is. The female orgasm is the ultimate point of creativity. Every time you get off, the waves of energy that come out from inside your body hot-wire the whole day. Having one or two orgasms every morning is a good way to announce to the world that your inner energy is more than willing to come out and meet it halfway.

Coffee, Tea, or Me?

Even if she has a whole brood of kids to pack off to school, every single woman I know sits and has her morning coffee or tea. It's a ritual. And you can just sit there and sip and let your mind wander, or you can use this morning ritual as an opportunity to bring your thoughts toward what you want to create that day.

Aside from all the things we know we *have* to do, we're all wanting and wishing for *something*. Maybe we're broke and need money. Maybe we wish there were more love in our lives. And sometimes we're in the middle of something that we wish with all our hearts would turn out the way we want it to. Instead of worrying senselessly about what *might* happen, or spending this time mulling over the logistics of the day, you can bring *yourself* into the act and transform this habit into something else altogether.

I keep a jar of cinnamon sticks on the kitchen table. From a magical perspective, cinnamon is one of those substances that covers absolutely every type of wish. And as I sip my coffee I stir it now and then with my little cinnamon wand. In between stirs, I can carry on a conversation or let my mind wander, but every time I pick up the stick to stir my coffee it brings my attention back to whatever I am wanting to focus on. The energy from those thoughts flows into my coffee cup and, on the way, the powers inherent in the cinnamon charge them up. As I drink in the coffee, every wish gets grounded and becomes part of me.

This works just as well with tea, and it adds to the flavor. If you're allergic to cinnamon, use a real wand. A vanilla bean is also good. And if you're one of those women who's in such a hurry that she has to pick up her morning beverage on the run, you can take advantage of the powdered cinnamon they now provide at every takeout counter or carry cinnamon sticks in the car with you.

Cleansing Ritual

Most of us take a shower in the morning, but you can perform the following magical act whenever you happen to be in the shower. This part of my day used to be as mindless and automatic as everything else I did. You probably all know what I'm talking about. And because our thinking processes never stop, we allow our thoughts to chase their tails without realizing we can do something else with them.

Now I use my shower to consciously focus my mind on clearing and cleansing myself of whatever I wish to be free of. This would include negative thoughts about myself, fears of whether I'll be able to handle everything the day will bring, overwhelming considerations about whatever is going on in my life, and anything else I might be too preoccupied with.

One of the best things about being in the shower is that you're *alone*. If you have kids, it may be the only point in the morning when there's a money-back guarantee that you'll have at least ten minutes all to your self. So instead of letting the "drunken monkey" in your brain run you around, see what happens when you give it something constructive to do.

After I get the water running, I step into the shower and rinse off. Then I raise my arms above my head and picture the water as if it's pouring down from heaven, instead of coming out of the tap. I connect with it energetically by sending a beam out of the top of my head. Then I bring my attention down to my feet and send a cord or an energy beam into the heart of Mother Earth. The image of the shower drain makes this very easy to visualize.

As the water pours over me, I picture it flowing *through* my body, carrying away everything that I don't want to bring with me into the day, carrying it all out through my feet, down the drain, and into the earth. While this cleansing process is going on, all you have to do is release the thoughts, feelings, and fears that might screw up the next twenty-four hours.

Don't be concerned about whether or not you're "doing it right." There's no wrong way to do this. And when you get out of the shower, you will notice that you feel lighter and clearer and freer. If you don't have anything specific to unload on any given day, you can say the following words, out loud or to yourself.

Shower Rhyme

Water of spirit, water of life
Flow through me now and carry all strife
Out of my mind and out of my heart,
Every new day is a whole new start.

Playing Dress-Up

Do you remember playing dress-up as a kid? My sisters and I used to do this for hours. We had a trunk full of secondhand prom gowns out in the barn, and sometimes the whole morning would be spent pretending to be queens, or princesses, or fairies. This was more fun for me than anything. I got so into it I actually *became* whatever I was pretending to be.

I am fifty-six years old now. Up until just a few years ago, what I wore every day didn't make much difference to me. In a way I deliberately tried *not* to focus on my appearance too much, because I had decided back in my twenties that it was vain. Well, I finally figured out that there's a difference between being vain and having a delighted awareness of your own wonderfulness.

I have also realized that outer beauty is a reflection of what's going on inside you. It's a reflection of the God within. And when you go out into the world looking your best, it gives everyone who crosses your path an opportunity to remember that fact, whether they're consciously aware of it or not. The truth about beauty is that it reminds us of God, and that's the *real* reason why we value it so much.

This revelation has freed me up to play dress-up every morning. The whole act of getting dressed has become a ritual that allows me not only to honor my own beauty but also to decide who I want to be that day.

After I get out of the shower and dry off, I feed my skin with moisturizer. I keep tons of essential oils on the shelf in the bathroom and, depending on what influence I want to attract into my life, I'll choose one and add a few drops of it to my body cream. If I want money I'll use cinnamon oil. For love I'll use rose or strawberry. When I just want to feel sexy I'll go for the musk. And I'll also use musk if I need to feel more powerful. If I "want it all" I'll use a drop of each oil.

As I rub this potion into my skin, I focus my mind and feel the energy of each substance infusing me with the influence that I wish to bring in. While I'm at it, I also send love and gratitude to my body for so willingly and graciously *being* there and supporting me in everything I do.

At the present time I happen to be doing private research into the whole concept of mind over matter and age reversal. So part of this anointing process includes mentally bringing my body back to a more youthful state. As I smooth the lotion into my skin, instead of looking at the wrinkles on my knee caps and thinking, "Oh my God! You're so wrinkled and old!", I catch the thought and turn it around. Now I say, "Your skin is so smooth and youthful. You are perfectly beautiful."

What we think has an impact on how we look, and we literally become our thoughts about ourselves. This isn't just New Age claptrap. It's a scientific fact. If you think you're old you will become old, because your mind has a huge investment in being right about whatever it thinks. So as you experiment with this preparatory, post-shower ritual, notice your thoughts and replace the ones that don't serve you with ones that do.

Once you're all "lubed up," you can do your face and hair with as much focus and intention as you put into the rest of your body.

When it finally comes time to put your clothes on, all you have to do is ask yourself, "Who do I want to be today?" Do you want to be Greta Garbo? Sophia Loren? Marilyn Monroe? Tina Turner? A princess? A fairy? A cowgirl? A witch? A queen? Do you want to look sexy or just powerful? Even if you wear jeans and workboots on the job, you can still look like a stick of dynamite.

You haven't forgotten how to pretend, so don't be afraid to do it. And what people see first when they greet you is your appearance, so if you look fantastic it will provide everyone with more incentive to get to know more about you. Besides, it beautifies the planet.

If you're one of those women who saves their nice clothes for special occasions, give it up! Every day is a special occasion. And it takes just as much soap to wash your ordinary clothes as it does to wash the pretty ones, so put them on! Get into this. If it seems shallow and superficial to you, it's not. It's just a simple way to honor and recognize who you are.

If you follow the little rituals I've described in the last few pages, by the time you leave the house every morning you will have called in the Guardians and received their blessings, focused your intentions, cleansed out all your hangups, turned back the clock, and created a more beautiful you. We have to do these things anyway, so why not make them magical? It doesn't take any extra time or effort, and it sparks up the whole day.

One last word of advice: don't get compulsive about this or you'll ruin it for yourself. You can give yourself permission to just be a slob if you want to. We're all perfect in our imperfection too, and just as lovable.

By the time you're ready to enter the day, the next thing you will confront is the trip to work. I have written a separate chapter for work and commuting spells, so you can refer to that for any on-the-go magic you might be doing on the job.

Sending the Kids off to School

For those of you who have children, the whole process of putting them on the school bus is a regular event that happens five days a week. As you send them out the door, you can use this part of your routine in a magical way too.

Our children are the physical embodiment of all of our creative energy. Every time they leave for school, it's very easy to visualize all your creativity blending with the forces that are active in the Unified Field on any given day, and to mentally honor that fact. Even if you drive your kids to school, or home-school them, the following rhyme can be used to help you turn this aspect of your life into yet another magical act.

Time for School Rhyme

As you take your books and walk out the door
I see my life and so much more.
Let your heart fly
And your spirit be free.
All you are is everything to me.

34

Evening

I don't know about you, but I love coming home. After a long day out in the world, it feels so good to re-enter the safety of my own space. And because at a certain level you're coming back to *yourself*, you can honor that very simply in a number of different ways.

Coming Home

I kiss the door before I open it. For me this is a way to say, "Honey, I'm home!" And I am making this statement to *myself* and no one else, because it's *me* I'm coming back to. Once I get inside, I strip off my clothes and hop in the shower to wash away all of the negative energy that may have followed me home.

Then I slip into something more comfortable and run my dogs down the path in back of my house. The dogs remind me that, regardless of what happened during the day, I am surrounded by unconditional love and total acceptance. If you don't have a dog, you might consider adopting one. They are like living furnaces that burn nothing but pure love for fuel. And the feelings they generate rub off on you somehow.

If cats do it for you, I totally understand. I love my cat too, but she provides a different form of energy than the dogs do. She is my "familiar" and is really tuned in to the spirit world. She-Ra is more like a live-in psychic than a pet. She's also my own private healer. I get treatments from the cat on a daily basis and have found that She-Ra's purring keeps me happy and healthy.

My kids are all grown and I am single, so I don't have the pressure of anyone needing anything from me when I walk in the door. For those of you who have people in your life, coming home is a different story. But you can still make it meaningful. Even if all you do is kiss the door before you enter, it's a magical act. Don't worry about the shower or having time to do anything else. It's unrealistic to think that anyone with a family would have any personal time at all in the evening.

What's for Dinner?

Cooking dinner can be magical too, if you know about herbs and prepare everything with intent. We cook up spaghetti all the time, but most of us don't realize that spaghetti sauce is a love potion. So is pesto. Anything made with Italian herbs and spices is a love potion. And the same goes for Mexican food. Hot peppers, cumin, and coriander all inspire lust. This *may* have a lot to do with why Latin lovers get such high ratings. There's an expression that says, "Food is love," and it's interesting that most foods, especially fruit and edible herbs, attract love.

If you want to keep your partner faithful, serve him or her rhubarb. When divorce is on the menu, work with turnips. A healthy serving of mashed turnips will ease whoever you're giving the boot to right out the door!

If you want to attract abundance, use cinnamon and cloves and all the traditional Christmas spices in your food. This will mean you'll have to start baking and serving dessert, or else get more into Indian cooking. Pesto doubles as an abundance dish, by the way, so if you want love *and* money, pesto would work as a main dish.

Tons of good books have already been written on the subject of "kitchen witchery," so I won't get into that here. It's a good idea for anyone who's into witchcraft to educate herself about herbs and spices and what their properties are. I'll leave that up to you.

When you get fully versed in this subject, your culinary activities will shoot up to a whole new level. The magical properties inherent in the food, along with the thoughts you hold while you prepare it, get grounded within you as you eat it.

As for the people who share meals with you, they don't have to be in on what you're doing. And as long as you're not feeding them evil intentions or trying to do them in with arsenic, it's perfectly legal to lace any meal with whatever suits your purposes. God knows, we could all use more love and abundance in our lives, and there's nothing wrong with filling your family with food that will inspire these things in their world too.

Be as relaxed and spontaneous about your magical meals as you are about the rest of your on-the-go magic. There's no need to get all uptight or serious, and you don't have to be in an altered state or cast circles for this to work. What you add to your food will create the effects that you're after, just because *that's your wish*. And as I said earlier, you have to cook supper every day anyway, so you might as well get as much as you can out of the routine. The whole point here is that there is magic in everything you do, and when you understand that, you get to a place where magic is *part* of your life, not separate from it.

Falling Asleep

Most of us are dead tired by the time we hit the sack, and I don't know about you but I look forward to getting into my bed at night. If you have a partner, there are a million different options to consider once you turn down the sheets. All of them are magical, and if you're in the mood you can approach them that way.

As far as going to bed goes, sometimes it's fun *not* to have to be too concerned with how conscious you are about it. But whatever space I am in, I always silently acknowledge that I am about to enter another realm. Closing my eyes on the day is always a prayer of sorts, because I am grateful for everything that has happened, and I look forward to being able to process it all in the dream state.

Reversing

Sometimes I do a process called "reversing" before I fall asleep. It isn't what you'd call "textbook magic," but its effects are magical as far as I am concerned. When you get really good at reversing, it can change your life. Here's how I do it.

After I get into bed and close my eyes, I mentally begin to *rewind* the events of the day, reviewing each one in a reverse sequence. Most of the time I drift off to sleep during this process. It's OK if that happens, so don't worry about it.

Reversing gives me an opportunity to stop at any interaction that didn't go well during the day, or any experience that didn't come out the way I would have liked it to, and change it. Once I untie the difficult sequences and rearrange the outcome in my mind, I see myself going through the revised version of the interchange three months in the future, making sure that I run through it as I *wish* to see it. When that visualization is complete, I continue going backwards from where I left off, stopping to rearrange things wherever I need to.

This process allows me to mend my life at the energetic level before I fall asleep. Reversing takes discipline, but if you get good at it you will see that it has wonderful effects that truly change your life for the better.

Unanswered Questions

I wasn't sure where to put this next part, because what I am about to tell you *actually* happens right before you wake up. The thing is, you have to prepare for it before you fall asleep, so I decided to put it here.

All of us have questions that we wish we had answers to. They range from, "Should I quit my job?" to "Should I leave my husband?" to "Should I go blonde?" to "Should I move?" to "Does So and So really love me?" There are millions of questions that fill up our minds, and we spend a great deal of energy wondering about these things.

Some of us even go to psychics and astrologers, hoping that they will tell us what we want to know. Paying people for this kind of information gets expensive after a while, and most of the time what we're told is inaccurate. The truth is that we have every answer we need right inside ourselves.

The following exercise isn't necessarily textbook magic any more than reversing is, but who cares? It *is* magic in a sense because it tunes you in to the part of your psyche that *knows* what the answers are. It's just like having your own crystal ball.

To do this you will need an alarm clock with a snooze button, a notebook, and something to write with. Set the alarm to ring half an hour before your regular wake-up time. Right before you fall asleep, pose any question you may have to yourself. (If you want to reverse, you can do that after you decide which question you want to focus on.)

When the alarm rings in the morning, grab the notebook and write down whatever you remember from your dreams. Then as you reach over to press the snooze alarm, repeat the question you posed the night before, out loud or to yourself, and fall back to sleep.

The alarm will go off again in ten minutes. When it does, jot down whatever you were dreaming about, repeat the question as you press down the snooze button, and drift back to sleep. You will do all of this one more time before you wake up for good.

By the time you get out of bed, the answer to the question you asked yourself the night before will be clear to you. Either you will "feel it in your bones" or the information you recorded from your dreams will hold the answer.

By now it's pretty obvious that there's no such thing as "not having time" to do witchcraft. Without casting a circle or raising a wand, you can turn everything you do into a magical act. You can even fix your life and tap into your psychic abilities while you sleep!

When you get it all down and really begin to incorporate what you know about magic into the routines that happen on a daily basis, being a witch takes on a whole new meaning. The truth is, it's *all* magic. You just have to give yourself the freedom to see it that way.

Chapter 3

Spells for Getting Around

Once we make it out the door, getting wherever we have to go is a different issue for each of us. We run, we walk. We go by car, bus, train, or bicycle. So much happens on the way to work. This is a major element in our daily routine that most of us overlook or totally take for granted.

Why we ignore the significance of this aspect of the day is hard to figure, when you consider the amount of time it sucks up. Some people spend an hour or more getting to and from the workplace. And there are a million different things that go on while we're engaged in this process. We have to deal with car issues, traffic jams, being on time, having enough gas, breakdowns, cops, road rage, snow, ice, bus schedules, train schedules, ticket people, conductors, toll booths, commuting acquaintances—you name it.

I have three really good friends who are tollbooth operators, and from what they tell me, they *look forward* to seeing the people who drive through regularly. Conversations take place, information is shared, gifts are exchanged, relationships develop, and sometimes they even end up dating their regular patrons.

The whole experience of being on the way to or from work isn't just lost time or wasted time. Things happen. Because *we* are there, *having* the experience, it's really just another area of our lives where we get to see ourselves, *be* ourselves, and notice how we are connected to everything.

If you're a witch there are all kinds of things you can do to make the time you spend getting from A to B more enjoyable and productive. I don't care if you walk, drive, take the bus, or use a broomstick, there's plenty of on-the-go magic that can be applied to this aspect of your day too.

The spells in this chapter are designed to make the whole process of getting around more fun and hassle-free. You can use any one or all of them whenever you feel like it.

Protection Magic

A little protection magic never hurts. Some people accuse you of being paranoid when you do this type of work, but to me it's common sense. Even though we all do our best to project energy that attracts positive experiences, we subconsciously sabotage whatever we're projecting for just because the human mind is polarized.

You can write affirmations till the cows come home, but the simple act of doing this implies that there's fear or lack supplying the fuel for it. If you're not 100 percent clear on every level of your being, the Law of Opposites will always prevail. And nothing can make you immune to accidents, speeding tickets, and breakdowns.

There are different ways to protect yourself while you're en route to or from work. You can use affirmations if you want to, but universal symbols and crystals are more effective. These things aren't subject to the same laws the mind is ruled by, because they embody the Oneness of the God force. That property renders them useful when you want to project a clear intention out into the Unified Field.

Since the whole idea of keeping it simple is important when you're on the go, I am going to make this as easy as possible for you.

Raido Rune

I work with runes a lot. These symbols are ancient, so ancient no one really knows where they originated. Over the years I have found that they have a tremendous amount of power and they function magically on a lot of different levels.

The "Raido" rune has many different meanings, but at the practical level this symbol serves as a form of travel protection. If you carve this image into a pocket-sized piece of wood, or draw it on a small, flat stone, you can carry it in your purse wherever you go. The energy inherent in the symbol fills your auric field–the emotional/energetic field that surrounds the human body–with safety vibes.

If you drive to work, you can keep this talisman right on the dashboard of your car or hang it from the rearview mirror. Another way to cover yourself, if the car is your main form of transportation, is to trace the Raido image on the hood of your vehicle with your forefinger before you take off to go anywhere.

Believe it or not, this is enough and as good as or better than more elaborate protection spells–your own magical AAA. The Raido image will not only protect you and/or your vehicle under any conditions, it will also help you find your way if you happen to lose it.

Crystal Protection

We talked about programming crystals back in chapter 1. Crystals have their own consciousness. They are *alive*. And I am pretty sure that they are a lot more on the ball than human beings are. We all have subconscious issues that sabotage our intentions regularly, so when it comes to travel protection I feel safer with a well-programmed piece of clear quartz than I do with my mental projections.

You don't need a big crystal for this. That's one of the nice things about these beautiful objects; small ones are just as powerful as big ones. I *would* recommend using an unpolished piece of quartz, however. Polished pieces are more beautiful to the eye, but the polishing process takes away too much of a crystal's innate power.

I mentioned earlier that every crystal has six terminations that meet at the point. To program a crystal for safety, all you have to do is hold *one* of those terminations up to your third eye and send thoughts or visions of safe travel into it. It's really very simple.

If you're one of those people who want to have all their bases covered, you can program one termination to eliminate mechanical problems, one to keep the cops from bothering you, one to make sure there are no accidents, another to help you run on time, one to protect you from weirdos, and the sixth one to make sure the gas tank is full at all times. For those of you who get to and from work via public transportation, on foot, or by bicycle, just adapt your programs to suit whatever your needs are.

Once the crystal is programmed, place it in a silk or velvet pouch and carry it in your purse or hang it from your rearview mirror. Many people hang "naked crystals" in their vehicles for protection. What they don't realize is that these things pick up all kinds of energy. The random effects of other people's thought forms can easily replace whatever you have programmed the crystal with. If you carpool with someone who has a particularly active energy field, his or her mental pictures can overpower your crystal's programming. So, keep it in a pouch. Even a hanky will do.

And make sure you clear and reprogram it once a month. If you have the time to clear your protection crystal with running water, by all means do that. If you're too busy, just blow on it. I usually do this at the new Moon, but if this is too hard for you to keep track of, do it whenever you can. A good time to clear things (and an easy way to remember that it's "that time of the month") is whenever your period comes!

For those of you who are unsure of your programming abilities, the following rhyme can be used to charge your Travel Protection Crystal.

Crystal Programming Spell

Wherever I go or happen to be,
The light from this crystal shines down on me.
No matter how near, no matter how far.
Nothing can harm either me or my car.

As you hold one of the crystal terminations up to your third eye, repeat the above ditty, out loud or to yourself, three times. If you're the forgetful type, write these words down on a slip of paper and keep it in your purse or glove compartment.

Life in the Fast (or Slow) Lane

Now that you're on the road, there are other things to consider. Like traffic. Up where I live, traffic is not a problem. In Vermont you can be on the road for an hour and not even pass a car! But if you work in an urban area, traffic is something you face all the time. Rush hour can be a real headache.

There's no such thing as serenity when you're traveling bumper to bumper at sixty miles an hour or more. It's impossible to do anything but keep your eyes on the road and your hands on the wheel. And you consider yourself lucky if things are flowing at a steady pace, because as stressful as this is, it's even more stressful when the cars *stop* moving.

Getting caught in a traffic jam is something we pray to God won't happen, but it's a daily occurrence for many of us. The problem with being trapped in a sea of automobiles is that you never know how long it will take for things to start flowing, and this generates all kinds of anxiety about being late.

A well-prepared witch is never at a loss in situations like this. Since there's absolutely nothing you can do about being stuck in gridlock, the best way to deal with it is to *use* the time. If you have relaxation CDs, pop them into the CD player. By the time you arrive at work you will be centered and clear instead of all wound up.

If you're *really* stuck, and it's obvious that things aren't moving at all, you can whip out your on-the-go spell kit and do a spell. I wouldn't attempt this if there were passengers in the car, but if you're alone, it's simple enough. I don't know about you, but I daydream while I'm driving. And my thoughts usually wander all over the place. If I had traffic jams to deal with, I'd certainly use the time to do a spell instead of just free-associating. Here are a couple of good love spells you can do while you're driving to work or caught in a traffic jam.

Apple Love Spell

What you will need:

An apple
A Swiss Army knife
A stick of musk incense

This spell can be done *while* you drive! Before you leave the house, take the apple and carve your lover's name into the skin. While you're at it, carve your name too. And it's always a good idea to draw a few hearts along with the symbols for Venus ♀ and Mars ♂. Wrap the apple in a napkin and stuff it in your purse.

Once you're in the car, light the incense. It's no big deal to store packages of incense in your glove compartment. Musk is all-purpose, but its reputation for being one of the sexiest scents makes it really good for empowering any love spell. Let the smoke from the incense fill up the car (if it gets to be too much, crack open the window). While this is going on, take the apple out of your purse and set it in your lap. That little spot between your legs is pretty powerful, and the apple will pick up any and all of the messages being broadcast from your hips!

Now you can start driving. Bring your mind and your heart to your lover, and focus your attention on what you would like to see happen, until everything is clear. When you have to stop and wait, or when you arrive at your destination, pick up the apple and start to eat it with intent. Eat the *whole* thing before you leave the car, seeds and all. The stem should be the only thing left when you're done. All the words and symbols you etched into the apple before you left the house will enter your body and help to ground the thoughts and wishes you're holding in your mind.

When the apple's all gone, toss the stem out the window. This will send your intentions to the Four Directions and etch them into the Unified

Field where all things are connected. Including you and your lover!

Quickie Love Spell

What you will need:

Your on-the-go spell kit
A tissue or paper napkin
A stick of musk incense

If you're at a standstill in the middle of a traffic jam, get a sense of how long it will take for things to start moving. If it's clear that you won't be going anywhere for at least five minutes, you can do this spell.

Light the incense. Open your spell kit and get out your bottle of musk oil, your Post-it notes, a pen, and your on-the-go crystal. Anoint your third eye with a drop of the oil and focus your thoughts on your lover.

When what you want is clear in your mind, write it all down. It shouldn't be a long, drawn-out thing. It's enough to say, "I want the connection between me and my lover to bring us closer together on every level." If you're single, you could say, "I wish to attract a lover who is perfect for me in every possible way." Dab the piece of paper with three drops of musk, fold it up, and place it on your lap for now.

Hold the crystal with one termination up to your third eye, and send all your intentions into it. Once this is done, set the crystal on your lap and keep your mind on whatever you're wishing for until the traffic starts flowing again.

When you arrive at work, wrap the crystal and the piece of paper in the tissue or napkin, and put this little package in your pocket or purse. After you get home from work, place it under your pillow and sleep with it there until your wish comes true.

Limitless Options

The Apple Spell and the Quickie Love Spell can easily be adapted for any other purpose. If you have money issues, success issues, or *any* intention that you would like to honor with a spell, follow the same procedure. Just carve the appropriate words into the apple skin, program your crystal accordingly, and write whatever you feel drawn to write on your Post-it notes. There's a lot to be said for making magic easy to do! The following spell, for example, is almost sure to come in handy.

Spell to Get the Traffic Flowing

What you will need:

Some bottled water
A stick of musk incense
Your on-the-go spell kit
A pen

Try this when you've absolutely had it with being trapped in a sea of cars.

Light the incense. Take a Post-it note from your spell kit and write down the name or number of the highway you're on. Underneath this draw a picture of the Laguz rune: ᛚ Like all runes, Laguz has many layers of meaning, but it is very useful in any situation where the "flow" is blocked.

Now draw a circle around the route number and the image of the rune. Close your eyes for a minute and picture the cars rolling forward.

When that image is clear, hold the bottle of water in your left hand and visualize it turning into a river. Once you have done this, open the car window and pour the water out onto the pavement. Things should start moving within ten minutes.

49

Bending Time

Being late is something everyone gets stressed-out about. There's a lot of anxiety when we're late for work because it makes us look bad. If you have to punch in and out, there's no way to hide your tardiness. It's also stressful when you're held up and you know you're going to be late for an appointment.

The thing about time is that it's an illusion. The truth is, it doesn't even exist. The past, present, and future are one and the same thing. That being the case, we live only in the present, and everything that happens is the result of what we *do* in the moment.

It's very easy to "bend" time. If you know it's going to take thirty minutes to get somewhere and you only have fifteen minutes, you can mentally stretch that fifteen minutes out to cover what it would normally take half an hour to accomplish.

I keep a rubber band on the blinker stem of my car all the time. Whenever I am running late, I take it and stretch it out, holding it under my thumbs across the steering wheel. Unstretched, it represents the time I appear to have. Stretched, it represents the amount of time I *need* to get where I'm going.

In essence, this little piece of rubber reminds me that whatever time I have is enough to cover the distance I need to travel. There's no need to speed or run the traffic lights or get aggressive about your driving. All you have to do is stretch that rubber band out and repeat the following rhyme:

White Rabbit Time Rhyme

I'm late, I'm late for a very important date,
But time does not exist and can't control my fate.

You will be amazed when you miraculously arrive on time at your destination! What I have found is that the clocks at my arrival point are not wound the same way mine are, or that whoever I'm rushing to meet is behind schedule too.

Road Rage

My ex-boyfriend used to go ballistic over the way other people drove. It had absolutely nothing to do with the traffic volume, because we were usually in the middle of nowhere. He just happened to have a very short fuse. When I was in the truck with him it was comical to watch him flip out over nothing. It also gave me an opportunity to observe the inner dynamics that fuel this type of craziness.

For most country people, road rage is a nonissue, but if you travel the main highways to get where you need to go, you're bound to run into it. If you ever find yourself wanting to kill the driver in the car next to, behind, or in front of you, take your finger off the trigger and use the following trick to cool down.

The Road Rage Spell

What you will need:

A stick of frankincense incense
Some bottled water
A roll of LifeSavers candies

When you're this ticked off, it's difficult to want to let it go. It may help you to reflect on what you're *really* angry about and realize that it has nothing to do with the passenger in the other car.

When you have to stop and wait, collect yourself enough to light the frankincense and let it surround you with peaceful, protective aromatherapy. Now slowly drink in the water and as you do, imagine it quenching the "fire" of anger inside you.

Once the water's gone, crack open the package of LifeSavers and suck on a red one (don't chew it). As you do, imagine that your rage is dissolving, and repeat the following verse over and over again until you calm down.

Rage Rhyme

No sense being angry at something so small,
Nothing this stupid can drive me up the wall!

If you happen to be on the receiving end of someone *else's* road rage, it's a different story. You need to deflect the negative energy being directed at you and protect yourself. The following spell works well in situations like this.

Psycho Mojo

What you will need:

A stick of frankincense incense
Your on-the-go spell kit, or:
A stone with the Algiz rune painted on it
A small pocket mirror

Light the frankincense and let those protective vibes fill up the car. If you don't have a stone with Algiz painted on it, you're going to have to get out your spell kit and draw it Υ on a Post-it note. This is not something you should try to do while you're barreling down the freeway, so you're better off keeping an Algiz rune on the dashboard. Algiz is a protection symbol and a good thing to keep in the car anyway.

Place the stone or the picture of the rune on your lap right near your Root chakra. This energetic vortex is between your legs in the perineal area. The Root chakra has to do with a lot of things, but it relates directly to survival issues.

Now visualize the Dagaz rune ᛞ on your third eye and imagine a bigger version of it around your car. This will make both you and your car invisible, and whoever is directing his anger at you will wonder where you went!

If your car is at a standstill for long enough, you can also perform the following antipsycho spell. Take out the pocket mirror and hold it with the reflecting face *toward* the angry driver. Mirrors have a lot of power, and in situations like this a mirror deflects the other person's rage or sends it back to him. Always keep in mind, other people's emotions belong to *them*. You don't have to be a target for this type of stuff.

Keep Algiz where it is, make sure your Dagaz imagery is crystal clear, and with the mirror aimed away from you, repeat the following rhyme out loud or to yourself until the psycho disappears.

Psycho Rhyme

You may be nuts but I'm OK,
Just back off and go away!

Give this a few minutes to work. Whoever has made you the focus of his anger will either pass you or get over it.

The Breakdown Lane

When you put protection magic to use, there is really very little chance that you will have car trouble. I am including the following spell "just in case." It will remind you that it's important for any woman who's on the go to educate herself about mechanical things. After all we're liberated, aren't we? And you don't have to be Mr. Goodwrench to fix a flat or know that if you toss a little gasoline into your carburetor the car will start.

Every now and then you wind up in a ditch. When there's an emergency of any kind and you're stranded on the highway let's face it, it's scary. Triple A is great, but those guys take forever sometimes. If you don't belong to AAA, you're basically stuck waiting for Godot. And with all the weirdos out there, you never know whom to trust.

My experience in situations like this has always been positive. I think these things happen just to teach us about the ultimate goodness of human nature. All the same, it doesn't hurt to cover yourself.

The spell that follows is for those rare times when you've broken down somewhere and have no idea how things will turn out or how long it will take to get rolling again. Make a copy of it and store it in your glove compartment.

Lady in Distress Spell

What you will need:

Your on-the-go spell kit

Get out your spell kit and dab one drop of musk oil on your third eye. Close your eyes for a minute and focus on clearing away your fear of being out of control. Once you're centered, take your Post-it notes and write the following words down:

I open my heart to whatever will be.
The universe always takes good care of me.
Help will come and save the day,
Someone wonderful is on the way!

Dab three drops of musk on your words and read what you've written out loud three times. Kiss the paper and stick it under the floor mat on the driver's side of the car. Before you know it, help will arrive and you'll be on your way again.

Parking Spots

I think everyone figured out how to materialize a parking place back in the seventies. In a lot of the crazy, New Age enlightenment systems that were so popular in those days, the first "mind over matter" exercise they taught you was how to create a parking spot. These exercises were in reality kindergarten magic dressed up as something else.

Those of you who already know how to manifest a parking space can skip this part unless you need a reminder. Some of you younger witches may have learned how to do this from your parents. If this is a whole new concept, don't be intimidated. It's a very easy thing to do and doesn't require any incense or paraphernalia.

As you approach your destination, picture the area in your mind's eye. "See" an open parking space exactly where you would like one to be. Don't be concerned about your ability to do this. With practice you'll become an expert. By the time you get where you're going, there will be an open space with your name on it, or someone will be backing out of a space just as you pull up.

This may seem absolutely too mundane, but it's not. When your life is busy it's a good thing to know how to do. Circling the block fifty times is a drag. And having to park a mile away from where you need to be is no fun either. If you're on the go, this is elementary magic that will give you one less headache, as well as extra time for more important things.

Time-sucking Voids

Whether we are on our way to work or out doing errands, there are people we run into every day whose primary issues cause them to suck up all our time and energy. You can always count on them to pop up when you're booked solid.

You can deliberately avoid these types if you're clever, but most of the time, you can't do anything but smile and pretend you're happy to see them. They hang out at the water cooler, the bank, the supermarket, and the gym, but you can expect to find them anywhere. They also love the phone.

I don't know what these people do when they're *not* sucking other people's time and energy, but it seems as if they have nothing better to do. Most of us are polite and kind enough to give them the space to do their thing. The problem is, the hour you spend talking with them is usually precious. You could use it to get things accomplished. It may even be the only time you have during a busy day to spend with yourself. Telling them you're overbooked and running late never seems to have an impact.

If you're on your way somewhere and you know you can't afford to get caught up with one of these people, you can always visualize the Dagaz rune on your forehead and make yourself invisible. It's quick, easy, and reliable. It works every time.

If you're already out and about and one of them happens to catch you by surprise, it's a whole different story. There's nowhere to run and no way to hide, so you have to use a different technique. The following trick is the best way I have found to eliminate the ever present threat of the Time-sucking Void.

Anti-syphon Charm

All you need to work this charm is a clear head. When you accidentally bump into these needy people, just remember that they're really there to talk about themselves, no matter how interested they may appear to be in you. Begin by asking them what's going on and get them on a roll. While they yap, you will have the freedom to focus your mind on something else.

In situations like this, visualizing the Isa rune | over a person's mouth works wonders. Isa "freezes" or stops the action of anything it is superimposed upon. You can even draw this rune with your right foot on the ground as you stand there. If you're leaning up against a wall, you can draw it on the wall with your right forefinger without appearing strange or odd. If you can keep your attention focused on the Isa image, you will see immediate results.

What usually happens is someone else comes along to interrupt the conversation. Either that or someone's beeper goes off. Sometimes your cell phone will ring. It really doesn't matter what it takes to do the trick, *something* will provide you with the perfect opportunity to make an exit and go about your business.

Walking

Maybe you get to work by walking. A lot of women walk for the exercise, and some of them fit this in during their lunch breaks. Anytime you're out walking you can kill two or three birds with one stone by making the walk part of your magical routine too. All this takes is the ability to pay attention and be mindful of what's going on inside and outside at the same time.

Even if all you do is focus on the movement of your body or your breathing, it can bring you back to your center. I have to walk my dogs four times a day, and I use these walks to clear my mind. As I move along I tune in to my true self and become one with the natural world around me. Sometimes I talk to myself about whatever's going on in my life, and I always pay attention to the rocks on the path.

You'd be surprised what rocks can tell you. So many of them have striations and markings that look exactly like runes. When I see a stone with a natural rune marking on it, I bring it home and take that symbol as my "sign" or message for the day. Inevitably it zeros right in on whatever the burning question is.

You don't have to be a mystical genius to work with runes. They are a very simple and direct divinatory tool. Go out and buy yourself a rune book. In time you will know all of them by heart and you won't even have to refer to it.

Walking on the Wild Side

I also pay close attention to the wildlife and the birds that come around during my walks. The crows tell me one thing and the blue jays another. If I see a hawk, an eagle, or a peregrine falcon, it's a major sign. Turkey vultures, wild turkeys, and great blue herons hang out where I live, and they have important messages too. Deer are a regular item, and every now and then I see a fox. Snakes and turtles cross my path. Even bees and wasps tell me things. So do the butterflies. When I walk at night sometimes I hear the coyotes howl or I see a possum. As far as I am concerned, none of this is random.

I pay attention to it because all of these encounters have meaning for me. If you're a city girl, there are wild things there too—pigeons, rats, mice, and cockroaches mostly! Or a spider in the shower. But hey! Even a cockroach has important things to say.

Any good witch knows that it pays to be acquainted with animal and bird symbolism. To help you understand it better, I am going to give you a short list of meanings, based on the wildlife I encounter when I'm out walking in Vermont.

If you want to get further into this, I would suggest you go out and buy *Animal-Speak* and *Animal-Wise,* by Ted Andrews. The book *Medicine Cards,* by Jamie Sams and David Carson, also has great information on bird and animal symbols.

Bird, Animal, and Insect Symbols

Ants—Ants are about community. They suggest that you need to develop a sense of closeness to the people in your community and work productively together. They're also a sign that it's time to stop fooling around and get down to work.

Bees—Bees have to do with working hard to pursue your dreams. They relate to your productivity level. Are you too busy or not busy enough?

Blue heron—The blue heron flies by when you need a day to yourself. It also gives you the freedom to be as eccentric as you want.

Blue jays—When you see blue jays there's a lot of gossip going on. People are talking about you behind your back, or *you're* the one with the big mouth. These birds address the idea of being bossy. Are you pushing your weight around inappropriately? Is someone else doing this to you? Blue jays also speak to the tendency to "dabble" and not take time to develop your talents as deeply as possible.

Butterflies—Transformation is the butterflies' message. They signify gentle, positive changes. They're also a symbol of hope and joy and tell us not to take things too seriously.

Chickadees–These cute little birds have to do with recognizing the importance of community. They tell you it's time to talk to your neighbors and visit with your friends. Chickadees also encourage us to be cheerful and to tell the truth.

Cockroaches–These creatures send the message that our survival depends entirely on being able to adapt in a hostile environment.

Coyote–Coyote says, "This is all just a game." He tells us to maintain a sense of humor and keep our eyes peeled at the same time. When you see a coyote, it means anything can happen. Big medicine is on the way.

Crows–Crows are about magic. They relate to what's hidden, and they know how to bring it to the light. They see the past, present, and future all at once. Crows aren't subject to human laws. They tell us to honor our own sacred truths and instruct us to be who we are. Crows on the left portend trouble. On the right they portend good things.

Deer–When these beautiful animals show up, there's always a lot of bonding going on. They tell you to be gentle and kind in all of your dealings.

Eagle–When you see an eagle, it's a sign that you have come into your own power. It's a symbol of leadership, vision, and a well-developed ability to hold onto your spiritual self and remain grounded at the same time.

Fox–Foxes have to do with being as sexy as you can. They also tell you that, for the time being, your survival may depend on your ability to play-act, or disguise your true intentions.

Hawk–Hawks are a sign that your higher self is guiding you. You can feel safe, knowing you're on the right path. When you see a hawk, you can be sure that there will be important messages and omens coming your way.

Mice–When you see a mouse, it's a message to pay attention to the small things. It means it's time to clean house, balance your checkbook, and get more organized.

Pigeons–Pigeons are a sign that it's time to find your way back home, literally or figuratively.

Possum–Possums hang upside down. When you see one of these little creatures, it's a sign telling you that maybe you need to change your perspective.

Rats–Rats are resourceful and intelligent creatures. When you see a rat, it's a message telling you that your success depends on making the most of what you have.

Skunk–Skunks address self-esteem and confidence issues. They tell you to be more sure of yourself. Sometimes they imply that you need to be able to pull this off without offending others.

Snakes–Snakes mean that big changes are afoot. Get ready for a transformation of some kind. It may be time to shed your skin.

Spiders–Spiders have to do with webs, connections, and networks. Whenever you see a spider, it's a sign that you need to get either more or less involved with others. They signify complications and entanglements. Are you weaving your dreams, or have you lost the thread that connects you to them? Spider imagery also speaks to the idea of creativity and is especially significant if you're a writer.

Squirrels–These little guys store things. When you see squirrels, ask yourself if you need to be saving something for a rainy day. Sometimes they tell you that you're being greedy, hoarding things, or being too acquisitive.

Turkeys–Turkeys are always an indication that gifts are on the way or that you will be giving something away.

Turkey vultures–This ugly bird is a really good sign. It says you are going through a time when you will be recognized more for the *value* of what you *do* than for how you look or what you have. They relate to the decomposition of old issues and to a period of purification that will lead to rebirth.

Turtles–This animal is a clear sign that you need to slow down and reconnect with the earth in an emotional way.

No matter how busy we are, the natural world is there in the background all of the time. If you're in too much of a hurry to see what's in the sky or on the ground, you definitely need a good reality check or a couple of weeks off! We all have eyes and can take in messages, whether we're power walking on our lunch break or sitting in the back seat of a limousine on the way to the airport.

Incorporating animal symbolism into your life is a way of acknowledging that you are one with everything and that the answer to every question is right in front of you. Get as familiar as you can with this stuff. Let the universe be your therapist. After all, it's free! And if you're on the go, observing the signs is way more cost-effective and time-efficient than paying a shrink to tell you what's going on!

I hope the information in this chapter has opened up your eyes to the countless possibilities that are available to you during the process of just getting around. When you're super busy it helps to know that you can make use of every minute. There's no excuse to not do magic. And the fact that you can incorporate it into whatever comes up while you're on the road makes that whole part of your daily routine much more pleasant.

Chapter 4

Witchery While You Work

All of us work. And unless we work at home, we spend up to eight hours a day somewhere else. Of course, the environment and surroundings we work in vary, depending on the type of job we do.

Some jobs don't allow you a whole lot of freedom to be who you are, and it's hard to find time and space to do anything but take care of business. Other jobs are set up in a way that gives you ample opportunity to do whatever you want. If you happen to be the boss, it's easy to get your secretary to hold your calls for an hour, or even take half a day off if you feel like it. If you're a waitress, a bus driver, a doctor, a nurse, or a day-care provider, adding magic to the work routine is a bigger challenge—but it *can* be done.

Jobs that involve constant contact with the public, and all the caregiving professions, keep your attention way too focused on the needs of others to put it anywhere else. However, regardless of how strict your situation is, you must get a break or two and at least half an hour for lunch. These little windows of time can be used to do spell work if you're clever.

One of the reasons I've decided to include this chapter on work witchery is that any witch who has a life needs to give herself permission to slip spells into the workday every now and then. If you've got a spell to cast and the best time to conjure things up happens to be in the middle of a workday, it's good to know that you don't have to wait till you get home to think about magic.

Many times, on a major cross quarter, I have so much else going on that I have no choice but to figure out how to honor the importance of the day in the midst of my other responsibilities. What I have learned from this is that spell work is just as effective when you don't have a lot of extra time to "suit up." It's far better to do what you can with the time you have than to blow your magic off completely.

The spells that follow will give you ideas about how simple it is to bring magic to work with you. Most of what's here will loosen you up and help you see that, no matter how busy you are, there's always a way to fit magic into your life.

Before we get into the actual practice of work witchery, however, there are certain things you have to know like the back of your hand.

Cross Quarters

There are eight significant days in the yearly cycle that every witch uses to do her most important spell work. They happen on February 2, March 21, May 1, June 21, August 1, September 21, October 31, and December 21.

On each of these dates a cosmic portal opens up. At these times, the "veil" that hangs between the real world and the spirit world is so thin that the whole universe is in a superconductive state. With so little resistance in the atmosphere, any magic you do will be twice as powerful.

If a cross quarter happens to fall on a day when you're too busy to think about it, it poses a conflict, because, for a witch, each of these dates has the spiritual significance of a major religious holiday. Not having the time to celebrate makes you feel as if you're missing something, the way anyone would feel if she had to go to work on one of her religion's holiest days.

It's too bad Wicca isn't recognized as a religion, so we could legally take these days off and honor our beliefs, the way other people do. The Inquisition put a damper on a lot of things, and we witches have had to figure out how to live with the situation. Fortunately, we're very adaptable. Amazingly, what got shoved underground so long ago is still alive and kicking, in spite of all the effort that went into burying it.

In the last few years I have been so overbooked on most of the Wiccan holidays that I've been forced to figure out how to honor them whenever and wherever I can. And I have learned that my spiritual survival depends entirely on my ability to bring Wicca into the realm that I live and breathe in. I don't separate it from my normal activities anymore.

As soon as I open my eyes on the day of a cross quarter, I ask myself, "What do you wish for more than anything today?" Coming up with the answer to this question is never a problem. There's always *something* to pump a little magic into.

Once what I want to do is clear, I figure out exactly how I can fit a spell into my schedule. I fast-forward the day to see where there will be openings or windows of time, and, within those constraints, I start thinking about what I will be able to do. When I know what the focus will be, I "tune" the spell to the specific vibration that's available on that particular cross quarter.

I'll give you an example of what I'm talking about here. Say I want to do a spell to attract love into my life. If it happens to be Imbolc (February second), I know that the energy in the Unified Field is perfect for holding and crystallizing thought forms. That being the case, my spell will revolve around "envisioning" the perfect partner and etching that vision into the aether.

If I were doing a love spell on Halloween, I would approach it from a totally different angle. On October 31 the energy in the atmosphere is more suitable for burying things that have been outgrown in preparation for a new beginning. The whole idea of burying things doesn't bring lovey-dovey pictures to mind, but it's perfectly kosher to do a love spell on Halloween if you know where to put the focus. A love spell at this time of year would involve kissing everything goodbye that prevents me from having love in my life, in order to create room for a new love to enter.

When you're on the go, you need to know what frequency each cross quarter vibrates at, without even having to think about it. To help you get a sense of what this means, I am going to give you a list to go by.

Imbolc–February 2: This is the time for seeding visions or etching thought forms into the universal matrix.

The Vernal Equinox–March 21: Time to fertilize the thought forms that were seeded at Imbolc, to impregnate ideas with male energy. Conception.

Beltane–May 1: Time to ground the fertilized visions into the earth, rooting them firmly at the physical level. Time to make them strong enough to grow.

The Summer Solstice–June 21: Time to recognize that the original visions are ready to bloom and become visible and tangible. Time to rejoice at the new life that has come into being.

Lammas–August 1: Time for celebrating the fulfillment of what began as an idea. The moment of perfection, being over-joyed at the end result of the creation process.

The Autumnal Equinox–September 21: Time to harvest and store the experience for future reference. Time for assimila-tion, integrating the original vision at the spiritual level.

Samhain–Halloween–October 31: Time to release everything that's passed, in preparation for what will come into being in the next cycle. Time for burying the old visions, connecting with the things that have to die in order for something new to be reborn.

The Winter Solstice–December 21: Time for the light to return and for the creation cycle to begin again. Rebirth of con-sciousness. Awareness of new possibilities. The first spark of light pierces the darkness and leads the way to the new vision.

A full understanding of how the cross quarters vibrate will become sec-ond nature to you after a while, if it hasn't already. A busy woman's magic doesn't leave a lot of time to think or plan in advance. You have to have all this knowledge at your fingertips and feel loose enough to be creative about what you do with it.

Now that you have an idea of where each cross quarter falls, mark those dates on your calendar so that you're ready for them when they roll around. Developing a sixth sense about whether the moon is new, full, waxing, or waning is something you need to get good at too. If you spend less time in front of the TV and more time watching the night sky this sense will develop naturally. Just so you know, *the sixth day after the new moon* is the best time to do spells that relate to expanding any type of possibility. Eclipses are really good for magic too. If you keep a good Wiccan calendar handy, it'll keep you posted on when eclipses occur and tell you exactly what the Moon is up to.

Simple Magic for Each Cross Quarter

The following spells can be done on your lunch break or even on a coffee break without a whole lot of hassle. They are being offered as guidelines, so don't feel limited by what I have come up with. Feel free to approach this any way you want to.

Imbolc Spell

What you will need:

Your on-the-go spell kit
Some milk (a half pint will do)
A tissue or a piece of cloth

When you wake up on February second, connect with the Four Directions and use your morning coffee/tea time to reflect on what kind of dream you want to install in the universal matrix. Keep in mind that these major openings in the cosmic portal are best used for your bigger visions. Don't waste this day on little stuff. Those things can be dealt with any old time.

Think about what really matters to you in the long run at this particular point in your life. Remember, whatever you envision today will be carried up into the aether and held there for as long as it takes for it to come alive.

Go about your morning business and do whatever you have to do to prepare for work. Make sure you bring some milk along or pick up a small container at the Quickee Mart. For those of you who are wondering, "What's up with the milk?" Imbolc is the day that ewes start lactating. In the dead of winter, this is the first sign that something is *alive* inside the belly of the Great Mother. And when her milk starts to flow, it means it's time to start using your thoughts to feed your dreams.

As you head off to your job, get an idea of when you might have space and time to fit a spell in. Keep in mind that you're going to need about fifteen to thirty minutes by yourself to get this done. When that time comes, get out your on-the-go spell kit, have your milk ready, and follow the instructions below.

Cast an energetic circle wherever you happen to be. Bring the four Guardians in. Place the milk in front of you and lay out the contents of the spell kit. If you can light a candle, anoint it first with the musk. If burning a candle is not an option, don't worry about it.

Dab a drop of musk on your third eye, get out your Post-it notes, and write your intentions down as clearly as you can. Once that's done, dab three drops of musk on the paper.

Now take the quartz crystal and hold one of the terminations up to your third eye. As you do this, read what you've written, out loud or to yourself, three times. Sit for a minute to make sure *all* of those intentions get "forwarded" into the crystal.

When this process is complete, take the spell that you've written and stick it in the container of milk. Wrap the crystal in a tissue or a piece of cloth and put it in your pocket. Thank the Guardians, send them back, and release the circle.

Now take a little walk outside and pour the milk with the paper in it into the ground. As you do this, "see" all those wishes going right down into the heart of Mother Earth. She will hold the vision for you for as long as it takes to come true.

By or before March 21, this spell will have run its course and you will know where things stand. In the meantime, keep the crystal under your pillow and sleep with it there. To cover yourself just in case you have other spells to cast, get a second piece of quartz to carry with you in your spell kit. (If you're a witch, crystals are like socks; you can't have too many of them!)

Vernal Equinox Spell

What you will need:

Your on-the-go spell kit
An egg
A pencil
A tissue or a piece of cloth

Picture yourself, waking up at dawn on the morning of March 21. Between now and the time you leave the house for the day, everything you do can be done from a place of wonder. Mother Nature's ability to rebirth herself and start again from the beginning every year is miraculous, and so is the energy available to you today.

Any or all of the "everyday magical acts" we talked about in chapter 2 can be used as you go through your morning routine. And what you need to be thinking about is the dream you seeded back at Imbolc. How far have you come with it? What does it need, and how can you bring it to the next level? If it's already come to pass, then there will undoubtedly be something else to work magic for, because that's how life is. What started as a thought on February second has developed into an ovum. And in order to evolve, this ovum needs to find its way to the womb.

Once you are clear about what you want to focus on, grab your egg out of the fridge, take a box of tissues or a piece of cloth along, and head off to go wherever you have to go. By the time you have your first coffee break, you may be ready to do this. If it feels as if there's not enough time, wait for your lunch break and follow the instructions outlined below.

Find a space where you will have enough privacy to work undisturbed. If the weather's clear and warm, you may even be able to take a walk and do this outside. Have your spell kit, your egg, your pencil, and your tissue in front of you, and cast a circle. If you are lucky enough to be able to do this spell outdoors, you can cast your circle with salt, pebbles, or sticks. If there's no time, or if you think you will attract too much attention, just cast it energetically. Call in the Guardians and quietly honor the Four Directions.

It would be great if you could include a candle in your magic today, but use your discretion. One way I have found to bring the fire element in without breaking any rules is to light one match at the beginning of a spell and let it go out. As far as fire goes, do what feels right to you.

Now hold the egg gently in your left hand and pour your wishes into it. When you're done take the pencil and inscribe those wishes onto the shell, using words or symbols of your own choosing. What you write will depend entirely on what you want to create. Wrap the egg in the tissue or the piece of cloth, dab three drops of musk on this little "blanket," and set the whole package down in front of you.

Using your Post-it notes, write down what you wrote on the egg a second time. You can use this as an opportunity to go into more detail or add thoughts that you forgot to include on the eggshell. When you're done read those words, out loud or to yourself, three times, anoint the paper with three drops of musk, and kiss it once.

Thank the keepers of the Four Directions, release the circle, and go find a place to bury the egg, the "blanket," and the paper you've written on. As you do this, see your wishes being held safe in the arms of the Great Mother and know inside that this act will bring them down to Earth where they will eventually become real. Once you're done, kiss the ground, and head back to work.

Beltane Spell

What you will need:

Your on-the-go spell kit
Some soil
A small flowerpot
Some seeds (your choice)

This is a very *physical* cross quarter. It's the day when everything we've been nursing at the abstract level gets brought into the physical world. Back in the days when everyone was still comfortable with the old ways, they celebrated Beltane by just going out into the woods and making love. It was pretty basic and simple. And as hedonistic as this seems to us, there was some substance and maybe even some hard physics behind this.

If you think rituals of this nature are just a way to justify wanton lust, your puritanical programming may be working overtime. Trust me. Try having sex in your garden on Beltane and see what happens to your crops. I guarantee your yearly harvest will be beautiful and plentiful.

Which gets me to my first point. You owe it to the universe, and yourself, to make love any way you can today. And if that's *all* you do, it's the best way to honor this cross quarter. Go for it first thing in the morning. And then, as you go through your daily preparations, bring in any or all of the everyday magical acts that we talked about in chapter 2.

What you want to be thinking about is your original wish, envisioned on Imbolc. If that dream has already come true, pick another one to work on. This is a critical day because what you've seeded at the aetheric level is actually going to enter the physical plane. The passage from one level to another is a very tenuous process, and you need to support it with all your heart and soul.

On your way to work get an idea of when and where you will be able to fit a spell in. When the time comes, have your seeds, your flowerpot, a little soil, and your on-the-go spell kit right there with you. If you can do this outdoors you may be able to build a circle with salt, or stones. But if you have to do it inside, or you think casting a circle will draw unwanted attention, cast an energetic circle and call in the Guardians.

Open your spell kit and anoint your third eye with a drop of musk oil. Sit for a moment and ground yourself into the earth by imagining a cord going from your Root chakra down into the heart of the Great Mother.

Take out your Post-it notes and write down all your wishes. Anoint the paper with three drops of musk and read what you've written, out loud or to yourself, three times. Kiss the paper once and put it in the bottom of the flowerpot. Fill the pot with soil.

Take a few seeds, hold them in your left hand, and charge them with your intentions. With your mind focused on what you're wanting, plant each seed, one at a time. If you want to, you can recite the following words:

> *Every wish will come alive*
> *As these seeds sprout*
> *My dreams will thrive.*

Send the Guardians back from whence they came, and release the circle. Bring your flowerpot back to work with you and, after you water it, put it in a safe place. You can leave it where it is or bring it home if that makes more sense. Pour as much love and care into this little pot of seeds as you can. Keep in mind that all your dreams are there. By the Summer Solstice they will bloom.

Summer Solstice Spell

What you will need:

Your on-the-go spell kit
A piece of red cloth big enough to wrap your crystal in
The pot of seeds you planted at Beltane, or:
A small bouquet of wildflowers and a jar to hold them

On the day of the Summer Solstice everything you have been dreaming about and wishing for becomes visible to the naked eye. And the point of this day is to *look* at what you've created and be joyful about the fact that the vision now has a life of its own.

It's a beginning in one sense, because what was at one point just a wish has entered the early stages of childhood. Like any mother, you have to be loving enough to keep caring for it, but wise enough to know that because it has a life of its own, it's going to go wherever it wants to from here. For the next month your job will be to nurse it and ultimately set it free so that it can give back to you whatever it came to bring you.

I consider the Summer Solstice to be both a beginning *and* an ending. We've reached a point of completion, so there definitely needs to be some celebration. But the moment of perfect ripeness is also the point at which everything starts to decay, so in reality this day is really the beginning of the end. The sun may be at its zenith on June 21, but what's less obvious is that its light is starting to wane.

You're honoring the awesome power of the life force and your connection to it on this cross quarter. In the spell work you do today you will be intentionally "blowing the breath of life" into whatever your wishes are.

If you had all the time in the world, you would be able to do this outside in the heat of the day and let the celebration go on into Midsummer Night. Most of us don't have that luxury. This spell will give those of you who have to work a chance to celebrate the beauty of this cross quarter with the time that you *do* have.

As soon as you wake up in the morning, connect with the Four Directions before you get out of bed. Stir your coffee or tea with a cinnamon stick, and think about what you want. Clear your body as you shower, the way we talked about in chapter 2, and go whole hog anointing yourself with lotion and any essential oil you want to add to it. I would definitely dress up today. Pick an outfit that says to the world, "I am happy to be alive and beautiful." This doesn't mean you have to get all trussed up in skin-tight clothing and panty hose. Be natural about it.

Before you head out the door, remember to bring along the plant you seeded at Beltane. If it didn't sprout, never fear. You can work without it. Pick a bouquet of wildflowers or stop at the grocery store and buy a few flowers. Stick these in your jar and bring them along to the job.

When the time comes to do your spell, have everything on the list above ready and cast a circle, one way or another. Bring in the four Guardians. With your plant or your bouquet there in front of you, sit for a moment or two and *look* at the miracle that's come to life. Get a feeling for this and write down whatever it is that you want the most on this day. Anoint the paper with oil and read what you've written. Tear it into little pieces and sprinkle them over the plant or the bouquet.

Now take the crystal from your spell kit and, holding one of the terminations up to your third eye, program it to foster the dream and keep it alive. Wrap it in the cloth and stick it in your pocket. Now, say the following rhyme three times, out loud or to yourself:

> *My wish is here,*
> *It's alive and well*
> *Where it leads me only time will tell.*
> *Every breath I take helps it to grow,*
> *I bless this process and let it flow.*

Take a deep breath and blow on the plant or the bouquet that you've picked. Thank the Guardians and send them back to their dwelling place. Release the circle and head back to work.

When you go home in the evening, transplant the plant somewhere on your property. If you can't do that, just keep it in the south corner of your house. If you used a bouquet to do this spell, bring it outside and bury it in the ground or toss it into the nearest body of moving water.

Keep the crystal under your pillow or in a safe and special place for as long as it takes for your wish to develop.

Lammas Spell

What you will need:

Your on-the-go spell kit
A bowl of ripe fruit, whatever's in season (cherries or peaches are best)
A hand mirror

Lammas, or Lughnassah, is basically like an award ceremony. It's a time when you get to recognize yourself for being such an incredible dreamer. On this day it's your turn to give yourself a big hand for what you've brought into being. If we don't take the time to *enjoy* what we've done, and we have no clue about how to celebrate the fact that *it came out of us*, what's the point of even living?

When this cross quarter rolls around, what you want to be thinking about is how incredible life is and, by extension, how incredible *you* are. It's not a tight, formal holiday. It's a time to rejoice and be happy. Spell-wise, even if all you do is go dancing at Lughnassah, you're pretty much covered. In a way, you're rewarding yourself just for being alive and being part of this wonderful thing called life. While this may seem frivolous, it's just as important as everything else.

No matter what I'm doing, I pretend I'm a movie star on August first. I imagine that I am giving myself an Academy Award for being human, and I dress up in my most beautiful clothes.

In the old times, everyone did this. The *Althing*, or the yearly gathering of the clans, took place right around Lammas. These gatherings were held in different locations in the British Isles, Scandinavia, Iceland, Greenland, and in the Northern European countries between July 25 and August 6 each year. Everyone came down from the highlands to show off whatever they had spent the year pouring their heart and soul into. It was no small thing–it was the "Althing"! And "All Things" participated in this celebration with every ounce of their being.

In the spell work you do today you're going to honor yourself. As you go through your morning routine put some extra enthusiasm into your "toilette." Anoint your body, fix your hair, and put on some makeup if you want to. Pick out something that you love to wear, and make sure you feel like a total fox when you walk out the door.

Bring along your spell kit, the fruit, and a hand mirror. Set the bowl of fruit on your desk or in your work area, and share it with your coworkers. When the time comes to do your spell, have all your stuff right there with you. Cast a circle and call in the Guardians as usual. Pick up the hand mirror and, as you look at your reflection, say the following words:

I am awed by who I am
And all the beauty that I see.
Everything in my life
Is a reflection of what's in me.

Open your spell kit and, using your Post-its, write down whatever it is that you want to create today. Anoint the paper with three drops of musk, kiss it once, and lay it facedown on the mirror. Now take a piece of fruit and, as you eat it, say the following rhyme:

Nature's gifts are just like us
They become perfect over time.
As I eat this piece of fruit
That perfection becomes mine.

Savor every bite and, as you do, imagine that you're taking in all of your own perfection. When you're done eating, save the pit or the seeds and place them on the piece of paper that you've written on. Take a deep breath and blow on the spell and the seeds and the mirror. Wrap the seeds up inside the paper and tuck this little charm into your pocket. Send the Guardians home, release the circle, and go back to work.

When you get home in the evening, bury the charm in the east, or toss it into a stream or river.

If you can go out dancing tonight, do it. Lammas is a celebration, and dancing is one of the best ways to feel the power of your own spirit at the physical level.

Autumn Equinox Spell

What you will need:

Your on-the-go spell kit
Some seeds (popcorn kernels will do)
A small pouch
A cup hook

September 21 is the point when we harvest and store whatever we've created so that it can be put to use in the future. All the experience from the previous year gets tucked safely away, or "put up" and preserved just like peaches in a mason jar. If we need that experience somewhere on down the line, all we have to do is get it off the shelf, take what we've learned from it, and put it to use.

The spell work you do today can be directed toward anything your heart desires. But behind everything you do, the thought will be, "How can I use the experience I have gathered so far to support this wish? Will what I know about myself provide me with the information that I need to bring this wish to life?"

In a sense you're honoring the fact that what's changed in the previous cycle has altered your understanding of yourself. The person who "saw the light" at the Winter Solstice and began seeding visions back in February has grown tremendously. And as you honor your growth, and symbolically "preserve" the knowledge you've gained from it, you also see that there's a much wiser witch at the wheel today. Because of all this new wisdom, *any* magic you do on this cross quarter will pack a bigger punch.

When you open your eyes on the morning of the Autumn Equinox, align your body with the Four Directions and connect with the Guardians. As you do this, ask them where the magical focus needs to be today. They will answer you in their own way, and this will guide you in your spell work.

As you get ready to leave the house, feel free to include any or all of the other magical acts we talked about in chapter 2. You need seeds for this ritual, and if you eat an apple for breakfast it'll save you the trouble of having to go look for them. I also use marigold seeds in my Fall Equinox spells because these little flowers are everywhere and they've usually gone to seed by this time. Popcorn kernels will do just fine too.

Figure out exactly when the best time to do your spell will be, and have all your stuff ready. When that time comes cast a circle, one way or another, and call in the Guardians to watch over things. Anoint your third eye with musk and dab some on your seeds too. Write down whatever it is you wish to create on your Post-it notes and wrap the seeds inside them. Place this little packet inside the pouch, and, holding it in your left hand, say the following verse, out loud or to yourself.

I am wise enough to know what I need
My life has taught me well
There's magic here in every seed
To fortify this spell.

With your eyes closed, send every thought you have about what you're wishing for into the charm bag. Hold the pouch over your heart center and see your wish coming true. When this process feels complete, thank the Guardians, send them home, and release the circle.

Head back to work and keep the pouch in a safe place till it's time to go home for the day. When you get back to your house, find a good spot to put a cup hook and hang your charm on it until Halloween. I like to hang my charm bags from the ceiling. You can also hang yours out of the way in the back corner of any closet. The point is to keep it safe because you'll be using this little item in your Samhain ritual.

Halloween (Samhain) Spell

What you will need:

Your on-the-go spell kit
The pouch from the Autumn Equinox spell
Some chicken bones (any old bones will do)
A small, cardboard box big enough to fit the pouch in
A piece of cloth big enough to wrap your crystal in

As far as cross quarters go, all of them count, but Samhain could be considered the most important one of all. Most people aren't aware of the seven other Wiccan holidays, but *everyone* knows about Halloween.

Back when the Celtic peoples were still practicing the old ways, October 31 was like what New Year's is to us now. It *still* marks the death of the old cycle and the beginning of a new one. If you're the least bit connected to nature it's very obvious that, in the Northern Hemisphere at least, everything dies in late October. And the period of darkness that follows is a necessary precursor to what will evolve into a new beginning by the Winter Solstice. Whatever we need to clear out of our lives in order to be ready for all the new influences that will filter in has to be taken care of, or we will remain stuck in the patterns of the previous cycle.

When you think about what you want to do for your Samhain spell, it's important to remember that you are simultaneously releasing the past and envisioning the future. As soon as you wake up on Halloween day, review how far you've come and acknowledge that everything you grounded back on May 1 has run its course. There's no way you can pump any more life into it.

And as you reflect on the idea of burying the past, you also need to ask your self, "Who will I be in the next cycle? What do I see myself becoming?" Once you figure out what that might be, go to your closet and choose an outfit that matches your vision of what you wish to become. You'll be wearing this "Halloween costume" to work today. The act of embodying what you want to be in the way you dress imprints that image directly into the Unified Field.

Include as many everyday magical acts in your morning routine as you can on this holiday. Have a clear idea of when you're going to have time to do your spell, and bring all of the ingredients for it with you to work. Don't forget to take the pouch you made at the Autumn Equinox off the hook!

When you're ready to get down to business, cast your circle and call in the Guardians. Anoint your third eye, the charm bag, and the bones with the musk oil. One to three drops will do.

Now get out your Post-it notes and write down what you want to release or say "good-bye" to. On a separate piece of paper, write down what you would like to become in the next cycle. If you have anything else you would like to focus your intentions on, you can include that in this spell too.

Take the piece of clear quartz and, holding one of the terminations up to your third eye, send the thoughts about what you want to become into the crystal. Wrap the crystal in the piece of paper that has that vision written on it, anoint it with a drop of musk, and kiss it once. Tuck this charm safely inside the piece of cloth and stick it in your pocket.

Take the piece of paper with the words that describe your desire to release the past, and place it in the pouch you filled with seeds at the Autumn Equinox. Put the charm bag into the cardboard box, lay the bones over it, and put the lid on.

84

Once all of this is done, say the following words, out loud or to yourself.

Everything dies when it's over and done
But new visions rise just like the sun
As I let the past go I open my heart
To the future, to life, to a whole new start.

When you feel ready, send all four Guardians home, release the circle, and bring your box and your crystal back to work with you. Keep everything in a safe place till it's time to go home. Once you get home you can either burn or bury the box with the pouch and bones in it. If you choose to bury it, bury it in the west, where the sun sets.

Take the crystal and find a safe place to keep it until the Winter Solstice. The visions you charged the crystal with will begin to materialize by December 21. At that point you can burn the paper and clear the crystal so it will be ready for your Winter Solstice spell.

Winter Solstice Spell

What you will need:

Your on-the-go spell kit
A stone with the Jera rune ᛃ painted on it
A small pouch or a piece of cloth

The Winter Solstice is a real turning point. This is the day the light from the sun returns and begins to increase day by day. The force from that light sets off a tiny spark that is way more powerful than the cold darkness that only *appears* to surround us.

I feel a tremendous amount of joy and anticipation on this cross quarter. The fact that *the light* is coming back reminds me that it's time to begin installing the vision that I see for myself deep within my heart space. And I know that I will spend the next six weeks getting clearer and clearer about what that vision is.

When you wake up on the morning of the Winter Solstice, make it your intention to *really* connect with the Guardians. Lie in bed and bring them in one at a time, and listen closely to what they have to tell you. Do the "Coffee, Tea, or Me" ritual, and as you sit at the kitchen table, allow your dreams to flow right into your cup. Drink this elixir in and *feel* those visions filling up every cell in your body.

As you step into the shower imagine the water as if it were light pouring over your body. Let this light find its way into your heart, and feel it as it circulates through you. Ask the Guardians to remove everything from your auric field that isn't "Of the Light."

Anoint yourself and dress in a way that makes you feel as beautiful and alive as you really are. This is a day when you want the world to see that something inside you is shining. If you like to wear jewelry, put it on just to remind yourself how bright and clear you feel.

You'll be using the Jera rune ᚼ in your on-the-go ritual today. Jera is sacred to the Winter Solstice. It's an open-ended symbol that signifies the point where everything turns around. It also embodies the idea that there's a divine spark in the empty space between one phase and another. This rune tells us to live from a place of radical trust and open our hearts to whatever will be. Before you leave the house, inscribe the Jera image on a flat stone, a piece of wood, or a piece of paper.

On your way to work, think about when you're going to do this spell. When that time comes have everything ready and cast your circle. Call the Guardians in and honor the Four Directions. Sit quietly for a moment, and, holding the Jera rune in your left hand, take a few deep breaths and remind yourself that you are nothing but light.

With your eyes closed, meditate on whatever you envision for yourself. Hold your on-the-go crystal up to your third eye and program it with that intention. Now place the crystal on top of the rune and anoint them both with a drop of musk.

Take out your Post-it notes and write down, in your own words, any thoughts you might have about what you want to create. Dab a drop of musk on the paper, kiss it once, and wrap it around the rune and the crystal. Hold this little packet in your right hand as you say the following words, out loud or to yourself.

As the light returns it shines on me
It glows inside me too.
My wish today willed be fulfilled
By everything I do.

Wrap the rune/crystal talisman in the cloth and hold it up to your heart for a moment. When you feel ready, send the Guardians home and release the circle. Head back to work and when it's time to go home bring the charm with you. Place it on an eastern windowsill so that every day when the sun rises, a little more light will shine on it. Within six weeks you will have a clearer sense of where your vision is leading you.

We've covered every cross quarter with "no hassle" spells that can be done no matter where you are. But remember, nothing here is written in stone. The best thing about being a witch is that you have all the freedom in the world to be creative and improvise any way you want to. The spells that are outlined in this chapter are meant to give you a jumping-off place. Whatever you wish to add to them is totally up to you.

Lunar Work Spells

Witches have always known that the Moon isn't just a lump of green cheese! She's more like a best friend or sister, someone who's there to help you out whenever you need her. It's a really good idea to pay attention to what the Moon does from month to month. Her energy is available to pump life into just about anything.

In between the major cross quarters there are always minor things that come up. And you can use the Moon to focus on your more "mundane" concerns *or* to nurture the dreams that you brought to life on the big holidays.

The problem with the Moon is that she travels very quickly. She moves one degree every two hours and changes signs every two days or so. Every week she's in a different quarter, and every two weeks she's either new or full. And then there's the whole waxing and waning thing. The Moon is a busy gal!

In the old days I did my best to keep up with her. Doing circles once a week in the traditional way was a full-time job. Even doing them every two weeks kept me on my toes. After a while it got to be too much.

One of the biggest misconceptions people have about witches is that they sit around doing spells all day. None of us is that neurotic. And if you're doing that much magic, you might want to consider managing your feelings some other way. If you're new to Wicca it's different, and it's OK to spend a year honoring every lunar phase. This is the only way to learn about magic and serve your apprenticeship, so to speak. But a veteran witch should be wise enough to get through life without having to resort to casting circles every five minutes.

Nowadays, instead of being a slave to ritual, I call upon the Moon only when I need her. If she's new, I know that I have two weeks to attract things into my life. If she's full, I know that I can use the power of her light to energize and fulfill any wish that's dear to my heart. As she wanes, I use that two-week period to dump or discard anything that isn't working for me. It's really pretty simple.

If you "have a life" it's inevitable that you're going to be busy whenever the Moon reaches these big turning points. If you want to do anything magical, you have no choice but to keep it simple and quick. We're living in a time when the expression "thoughts have wings" applies more than it ever did. So it's fine to sit quietly with your eyes closed, send your intentions out into the Unified Field, and trust that the lunar forces you're tapping into will take it from there. Going into your heart and feeding your intentions from that place is just as good as doing a spell, believe it or not. And if that's all you have time for, it's enough.

The spells that follow can be done anywhere, and they can be applied to any purpose. You can pull them out on the spur of the moment without having to think about it too much. When you're over-booked or overwhelmed and suddenly remember that the Moon is new, full, or waning, you don't have to say, "Gee, it's too bad I don't have time. I would love to do a money spell."

Busy witches know that there's more than one way to skin a cat!

New Moon Spell

What you will need:

Your on-the-go spell kit

When the Moon is new, the focus is always on drawing things *to* you. This little spell will work to attract love, money, success, beauty, or whatever it is that is specific to your needs at the time. You can do it at the office, on your lunch break, on your coffee break, or even in one of the stalls in the ladies' room! If you're on the road you can stop at any highway rest area and do it.

Start by casting an energetic circle, and call the Guardians in. Focus on your breathing and slow your mind down enough to formulate your wish. Hold the crystal up to your third eye and say the following words, out loud or to yourself.

My deepest wish is real and true
The Moon will make it shine
As her light grows my dream will too,
And what I desire will be mine.

Send your vision into the crystal and, when you're done, hold it up to your heart. Wrap it up in a Post-it note and stick it in your pocket or purse. Thank the Guardians and release the circle. When you get home, sleep with the crystal under your pillow until your wish comes to life. Make sure you clear the crystal before you do your next spell.

Full-Moon Spell

What you will need:

Your on-the-go spell kit

The full Moon is good for amplifying anything you wish to focus on. It's the best time to send your deepest desires out into the universal matrix. There's no need to worry about having enough time. This spell only takes a few minutes, and you can do it anywhere.

Cast your circle energetically and connect with the Four Directions. Dab a drop of musk on your third eye, close your eyes, and say the following rhyme out loud or to yourself.

Lady Moon shines for me
She knows just what to do.
My wish is bigger than it will ever be
And I know it will come true.

Dab a drop of musk on your heart center. Now focus your mind on what you want and say it out loud. Even if you have to whisper, let your words filter out into the Unified Field. Repeat the above rhyme once more, thank the Guardians, and release the circle.

Waning-Moon Spell

What you will need:

Your on-the-go spell kit

When the Moon is in her waning phase, you have two weeks to release anything that you don't want in your life. You can get rid of old habits, nasty people, old flames, and negative thought forms at any time between the day after the full Moon and the day before the new Moon.

As you're traveling down the highway or sitting at work thinking about how much you would love it if you weren't stuck with something you don't want, instead of wishing it away, you might want to consider doing the following spell.

Cast an energetic circle and call in the Guardians. Anoint your third eye with a drop of musk and get out your Post-it notes. In your own words, write down exactly what it is that you would like to eliminate. Hold the piece of paper up to your third eye and "see" this as if it were already true. Now take the paper and, holding it in your left hand, say the following words, out loud or to yourself.

This issue (person, habit) no longer troubles me
As the Moon fades so it (they) will too.
By the time She is New again,
This problem will be through.

When you're done reciting this rhyme, draw an X over what you've written and spit on the paper. Thank the Guardians and release the circle. On your way back to work, rip the paper up and flush it down the restroom toilet! Whatever you're wishing away will go down the drain by the next new Moon.

If you happen to be out in the middle of nowhere and there are no toilet facilities, all you have to do is rip the paper up into tiny pieces and toss it to the four winds.

So there you have it—magic that comes to work with you. We've covered every cross quarter and lunar possibility with magical options that don't require any time or fancy accoutrements. It might be a good idea to keep a copy of this book in your car or at work until you feel more comfortable with your on-the-go spell work.

I have a feeling that once you get the hang of it, you'll realize that the spells written here don't have to be followed to the letter. You can make up your own spells. Magic is art after all, and way more powerful when you create it yourself instead of painting by someone else's numbers.

Chapter 5

Witch on Vacation

It seems as if there's some sort of conspiracy that keeps us all running around like wind-up toys. Whoever sold us the idea that working, driving around in cars, going to the bank, and being exhausted by it all is where it's at must get a kick out of knowing that no one on the planet has time to think anymore. Witches are just as sucked in by these forces as everyone else is. When you're constantly on the go, it's easy to forget what's important.

Kissing your everyday routine goodbye is just as necessary as all the things you do to keep it going. A heavy dose of peace and quiet and the freedom to reflect brings you back to center. And you can just lie around all day if you want to. But while you're sunning yourself at some fancy resort, there's no rule that says you can't bring yourself together at the spiritual level too. If you're a witch there's nothing odd about doing magic while you're on vacation. The truth is, there's no better time for it, because you finally *have* time!

Where do we go when we take off for a week or two? We head to the beach, or off to a resort. Some people hop on a boat and take a cruise. We travel to other countries. In the winter we go skiing and spend time in the snow. Some people go on "spa vacations," and others go out into the wilderness to camp. Regardless of where we take off to, every vacation spot provides a perfect setting and plenty of time for spell work.

Like all the spells in this book, the ones that follow are meant to remind you how easy it is to bring magic wherever you go. I have tried to gear them to every vacation scenario I can think of.

We're going to start with the beach, so pack up your on-the-go spell kit and let's pretend we're heading off to spend a couple of weeks at the shore.

Beach Magic

Whether we know it or not, the whole reason everyone loves to go to the beach is that all four elements are right there. The fiery heat of the sun, the warm sand, the cool ocean breeze, and the blue water surround us with fire, earth, air, and water. Something inside us *needs* to be nurtured and healed by these forces. We're at one with life whenever we're at the seashore, and if you're a witch, it's the easiest place in the world to do magic.

If you're all by yourself on your blanket, a week by the sea can be one long magical act. But even with a pile of kids and all kinds of activity, you can turn your vacation into more than just a picnic if you know what to do.

Even though most people like to sleep late while they're on vacation, we're going to start with a sunrise spell. Sleeping in is fine, but after the first few days, it's so exciting to have all the time in the world that waking up at dawn is a treat.

You can do this spell every morning. The purpose here is to wash away every bit of stress and care, but you can also use this little ritual to focus your intentions on anything else your heart desires.

Sunrise Spell

What you will need:

Your on-the-go spell kit
A votive candle
A jar to put the candle in
A stick of incense (your choice)
A stick

Head down toward the water and figure out which direction is where. This shouldn't be too difficult, because the sun rises in the east. Set all your paraphernalia in one spot. Starting at the north, and moving in a clockwise direction, draw a circle in the sand with your stick.

Once the circle is drawn, go to the north and, standing with your arms raised, call in the Guardian of the Watchtower of the north. Go to the east, south, and west and invoke all of the Guardians, one at a time in the same way. Now go to the north quarter and walk around the inside perimeter of the circle three times to seal it.

Sit down in the center of the circle and either face the ocean or any of the Four Directions. Which direction you choose is up to you. Trust your instincts.

Anoint the candle, wick to base, with the musk oil, set it in the jar, and light it. Use the candle flame to light the incense, and stick it in the sand. Dab a drop of musk on your third eye and close your eyes. Slow your breathing down and imagine that you are inside your heart. After a few minutes say the following words out loud:

Sunrise Rhyme

As the sun comes up all darkness fades,
It goes out with the tide.
My heart is full of solar light
I feel it deep inside.

Listen to the rhythm of the waves and tune your breathing to the sound of the ocean. Stay within yourself for as long as you want to. When you open your eyes, if there is something you would like to focus on, get out your Post-it notes and write it down. Read what you've written out loud three times, kiss the paper once, and either bury the paper in the sand or burn it to ashes with the flame from the candle. Use your discretion as far as burning goes.

When you are done stand up in the center of the circle. Using the stick as a wand, hold it up to the sky and turn around clockwise three times. Go to the north, east, south, and west, thank each of the Guardians, and send them home. Snuff the candle out in the sand and release the circle by sweeping it away with the stick.

If you're in the mood, the best way to finish off a spell like this is to jump in the water and go for a swim. It'll help to cleanse and wash away everything that keeps you out of touch with who you are.

Magical Picnic with the Kids

A lot of us have kids, and they go with us wherever we go. If you're on vacation with your children, the best way to make magic is to *be* with them. Kids are tuned in to life much more than adults are, and they can teach you a lot about just *being*. When you're in that space, you're one with absolutely everything and it's already enough. You don't have to intellectualize these moments in time or "witchify" their perfection by trying to do spells. You don't have to *do* anything but *be* there with your little ones.

Keep in mind that your own inner child wants to come out and play too. The whole reason you take a vacation is to give it some airtime. So stop obsessing about how you look in a bathing suit and don't worry about whether you're going to have time to read your trashy novel. Forget about having enough time to lie quietly and tan, too. Pick up a pail and a shovel and go make drip castles with your kids. Play in the water and when you get sick of that, go collect shells. There's enough magic in the pure simplicity of things like this to let your day at the beach just be about your inner child.

At the same time, there are things you can do that will add a magical element to any day at the beach with your children. The best thing to do is spend as much time as you can in the water. Seawater is like amniotic fluid. Whether we're aware of it or not, we all go back to the womb when we're at the ocean. That's what the sea represents to the subconscious mind. If your kids are little enough to enjoy splashing around with you, have them take turns getting held in your arms and rocked in the waves.

This isn't textbook ritual by any means, but no one who's done it once will doubt that there's something magical about it. Try it and you'll see what I mean. Getting baptized in the waters of life by your mother, your grandmother, or your father is a wonderful healing experience for everyone involved. Believe me, you won't ever forget it, and neither will they.

The other thing you can do–and your kids might enjoy doing this too–is arrange the four corners of the beach blanket to face the Four Directions. Once it's all lined up, go to the north, east, south, and west and mark each point with a stone or a shell. See if the kids like the idea of laying their towels at each of the quarters, and let them pretend to be the Guardian of that direction.

Once everything's arranged, go out and gather all the beach rocks, shells, or beach glass you can find, and make a circle around the blanket. Give yourself plenty of room. Make the circle big enough for everyone to move around. This creates a sacred space. Believe it or not, it will insulate you against all of the craziness getting dispersed by the less ethereal types blasting the radio on the blanket next to you.

You can also take the time to create a picnic lunch that will nourish both body and soul. Have your basket well stocked with apples and pears and magical fruits. Bring along some clear spring water or apple juice. Remember to add witchy herbs to your sandwiches. Throw a little basil and some oregano into the tuna or the egg salad. Add some tomato, too. All these ingredients are carriers for feelings of love and fulfillment. Use wheat or rye bread to amplify those feelings.

As far as dessert goes, the fruit will do. But if you really want to go for it, here's another idea. One of the fun things witches do is serve "cakes and wine." Pop a wine cooler in the basket for yourself, and let the juice be for the kids. For treats bring shortbread or cupcakes. When it's time for dessert, gather on your beach blanket and have a little toast to life, or joy, or whatever you want to make a toast to. Let your children decide what they want to honor. And then enjoy the taste of the cakes. Feel them going down and be reminded that it's *life* you're taking in.

You don't have to make a big deal out of any of these magical acts. What I mean is, don't feel compelled to explain what you're up to. And forget about teaching the kids about Wicca! This isn't Sunday school!

Your children have their own path. And if at some point in their lives they *do* get into Wicca, they'll look back on the picnics at the beach and smile.

Keep it light. Keep it simple. It's better that way. Once you get into the swing of things, you'll come up with your own way to bring magic to the beach, because that's what happens when you let your inner child come out to play.

What If You're All by Yourself?

Ask any witch on the go how she likes the idea of spending a week or two alone at the beach, and I'll bet you she'll say, "It sounds like heaven!"

Taking a beach vacation by yourself is like having a spa retreat. The entire experience is about *you*. And you can do any kind of magic that you want to, as long as you promise to keep it fun. After all, you came to relax and get a little sun, and you shouldn't be concerned with doing anything you're not in the mood for.

Find a spot where you feel at home, and create a sacred space by lining your blanket up to the Four Directions. Mark each quarter with a stone or shell. Give yourself plenty of room to spread out and, moving from the north in a clockwise direction, draw a circle in the sand with your foot. Once you set up your beach gear, align your body with the Directions and, when you feel ready, call in the Guardians, one at a time.

From this point on, the day is all yours, and what you do is totally up to you. But I would suggest you spend a lot of time floating around, swimming, or wading in the water. Let the ocean wash your spirit clean, and allow the sun to fill your heart. The only thing you need to remember is, whenever you get up to go swimming, make sure not to step on the circle you've drawn in the sand. You don't want to upset the balance you've created inside this sacred space.

If there is anything in your life that you want to improve or change, part of the day can be used to focus your intentions on it. The spell that follows is in the form of a rhyme or mantra. It suits any purpose. You can say it while you're lying in the sun, floating in the water, or walking along the shore. All you have to do is repeat this out loud or to yourself at least three times, whenever you think of it.

All Alone Rhyme

My life is like the sea
The way it flows is a sign
When I just let everything BE
Whatever I wish for is mine.

If this seems too simple, remember, thoughts have wings and words have power. There's no strict ritual here, but things like this work as magically as anything else. You can add whatever you want to the equation, but what's here is enough.

When you're ready to head home for the day, all you have to do is mentally send the Four Guardians back and erase the circle with your foot.

Magical Times Vacationing with Your Lover

I am including this because if I don't, someone's going to wonder why I didn't. If you're vacationing *anywhere* with your lover, my advice is— leave the spell book at home. It's ridiculous to do spells when you're *honeymooning* with your one and only. Spend as much time making love as you can, and consider it magical enough. This is what all of us live for and dream about, so just relax and have a good time.

Sundown Spell

What you will need:

Your on-the-go spell kit
A votive candle
A jar to put the candle in
A stick of incense (any kind will do)

Every time the sun moves over the western horizon we sweep away the day and put it to rest. At this hour it's probable that you'll have the beach all to yourself, but if you don't, find a nice quiet spot where you won't be disturbed.

With your magical equipment in place, make a circle in the sand with your foot. Mark off each of the Four Directions with a stone or a shell. Call in the Guardians, starting at the north and then going to the east, south, and west. If there are people around, and you don't wish to appear odd, you can invoke the spirits in a whisper or energetically.

Sit down in the center of the circle and face the west. Anoint the candle, base to wick, with some musk, set it in the jar, and light it. Spark up the incense and stick it in the sand. Anoint your third eye and close your eyes. Breathe to the rhythm of the waves and, when you feel ready, say the following words out loud:

Sunset Rhyme

Cleanse my heart of all my cares,
Let them leave this shore
As the sun goes down and fades away
My soul is free once more.

Repeat this rhyme three times and remain still, with your eyes closed. Let the sounds of the evening and the ocean breeze fill you with peace and calm. When you feel ready, open your eyes and gaze at the candle flame. Go into your heart and ask for whatever it is that you need or want. Make believe that the light from the candle is there to give life to all the things you are feeling right now. Imagine that this light will stay with you and be there to energize your dreams in the morning.

When the time is right, send the Guardians home and sweep away the circle with your foot. Carry the candle in its jar back to your hotel room and leave it burning next to your bed all night. To be on the safe side, be sure to place it away from curtains or any other flammable item in the room.

All of these magical acts can be used wherever you go. They work just as well in the south of France as they do in Alaska! If you're vacationing near a lake or a river, or even at a swimming pool, they can be done just as easily there. You can even do them on the deck of a cruise ship if you use your imagination. You may have to modify the way you build your circle, but you can always cast an energetic circle if there's no other way to do it.

Row, Row, Row Your Boat

Water is the universal solvent. It's also a superconductor. If boating is what you do when you're on vacation, it will help to remember that you can do all kinds of good magic while you're floating around. The superconductive properties of water make it the ideal transmitter for any type of wish. This isn't just some metaphysical notion. So much research has been done on water lately that even the scientists know that it both receives and transmits emotion.

Unless you're on an ocean liner, your space will be limited. Most sailboats and cabin cruisers are pretty compact, and canoes–forget about it–

there's no room to do much of anything. The spell that follows is remarkably simple and geared toward any type of wish. The next time you're out on the water and you feel peaceful enough to do a little magic, pull it out of your bag of tricks and see what happens.

Water Spell

What you will need:

Your on-the-go spell kit

Before you step on board, it might help to write down what you want on your Post-it notes. Those of you who are overnighting or living on the boat for more than a day or two won't need to do this. But if you're canoeing or white-water rafting, it'll be easier to do your writing in advance and have your wishes tucked safely in your pocket.

When there's enough peace and quiet, and you're clear that all of your companions will be minding their own business for at least ten minutes, you'll be ready to start.

Cast an energetic circle. Picture it rippling outward in concentric rings around the boat. Tune to the Four Directions and, beginning at the north quarter, move to the eastern, southern, and western quarters in turn, bringing all of the Guardians in.

Slow your breathing down and bring your mind into the moment. Listen to the water and feel the wind blowing softly around you. If you're close enough to touch the water, wet your hand and anoint your third eye with a few drops of H2O. Those of you who can't reach the water can lick your finger and anoint your forehead with saliva. It's not quite the same, but remember, when you're floating on *any* body of water, you're in a superconductive medium that connects all things.

Focus your mind on your wish. If you haven't already written it down, go ahead and do it. Now draw the Laguz rune ↾ in the air with your finger. Trace it over the paper, and over your third eye too. Laguz is a water rune. It has a female vibration and tunes you in to the creative flow of your intuition and innate psychic abilities. With all the power of your focused intentions, say the words that are on the paper out loud or to yourself, and then repeat the following rhyme:

Water Rhyme

Floating up from deep inside
My wish comes up to meet the tide
It surfaces and lets me see
That whatever I want will come to me.

Sit for a moment and feel your heart beating. Let your wish center itself inside your heart. When you feel ready, cast the piece of paper into the water. The words will mix with the universal solvent, and whatever you're wishing for will be broadcast into the Unified Field. You should have exactly what you want before you know it.

To close this spell, all you have to do is start at the north and move clockwise. After you thank all of the Guardians and send them home, release the circle.

Mountain Magic

Some people "head for the hills" and go off to the mountains when they vacation. It's so moving to be way up, close to the sky. Mountains are huge power points. And there's a different kind of energy there than there is anywhere else. It's awesome to envision the minerals, crystal formations, and invisible fissures all piled up inside these earth castles. Every mountain is like a gigantic breast that you can draw a lot of earthly and heavenly power from at the same time.

Watching the sun rise and set is a peak experience when you're on a mountain retreat. I would suggest that you crawl out of bed every morning and take the time to "make your day" by watching the sun come up. And if you can sneak away at sunset to watch it go down and put the day to rest with a spell, it will definitely help to keep you centered. The Sunrise and Sunset Spells in the "Beach Blanket Bingo" section can be easily adapted to higher elevations. All you have to do is build and release your circle differently.

The most truly amazing thing about the mountains is the way the sky and the stars look at night. I have often been moved to tears and filled with wonder by this sight. The following spell is for all you on-the-go gals who have been too plugged into the rat race to even look at the stars. If you're hanging out in the mountains, you'd be a fool not to tune in to them with this little spell.

Heaven and Earth Spell

What you will need:

Your on-the-go spell kit
A votive candle
A jar to put the candle in
Some incense (optional)

Sometime after dark, when the stars finally come out, find a place where you feel safe and cast an energetic circle. Starting at the north point and moving clockwise, go to each of the Four Directions and call in all the Guardians.

Stand or sit in the center of the circle and anoint your candle, wick to base, with a few drops of musk. Set the candle in the jar and light it. If you're using incense, spark it up with the candle flame and stick it in a crack between the rocks next to you.

The flame from the candle and the smoke from the incense are a signal to the greater universe that you are here and part of everything. Sit quietly for a few moments and contemplate this. Take in the beauty of the night sky and the awesome silence surrounding you. Open your heart completely.

When you feel ready, anoint your third eye with a drop of musk and say the following words out loud with your eyes closed.

Night Sky Rhyme

Sitting here beneath the sky
I open my heart and ask it WHY
I came to be.
I know I was born to serve God and man
But tonight I want to hear
The voice that can tell me clearly
Where I fit into the plan.

Stay where you are with your eyes closed and listen to your heart and to the overwhelming silence that fills the space between heaven and earth. If it has something to say, let your inner voice speak to you. When you feel ready to open your eyes, do so.

From this point on, all you have to do is take in the energy from the rocks beneath you and the stars above you. There is no way I can tell you how to do this except to say that there is a cord flowing through your spinal column that connects you to the earth and the sky. Extend that cord down into the core of the planet and send it up into space, to touch whatever is at the source. Once you've done that, breathe in a way that brings heaven and earth *together* inside your heart.

What happens when you do this will be unique to you. Just be as open as you can to the messages you receive, and trust that this information is real. When you feel complete, go to the north point, send each of the Guardians home in succession, and release the circle. Carry the candle back with you to wherever you're staying, and let the flame burn next to your bed all night.

This little spell will take you very deep inside yourself. It will empower you with a deeper understanding of who you are and what your life is really for. When you return to the rat race, your perspective will be entirely different. Whatever you heard or felt when you were on top of the mountain will stay with you for a long time.

Hiking and Biking Trips

I am not a big hiker or biker or sports enthusiast. For twenty-one years of my life I was so addicted to exercise I ended up overdosing on it back in 1992. But a lot of people love to get physical, and they use their vacation time to get into these things.

When you're hiking or mountain biking in the wilderness, there are usually other people around and too much movement involved to do spell work. But you *can* do what I call a "mantra spell."

Mantra spells are repetitive rhymes that you can say over and over again to yourself, no matter what your body is doing. They make it possible to do something constructive with your mind and heart while the physical you is otherwise occupied.

Here's a simple mantra spell that you can take anywhere. It's quick, it's easy, and anyone whose vacation time includes a lot of exercise will find it useful.

You don't need anything but your own voice for this. All you have to do is repeat the following rhyme, out loud or to yourself:

Witch in Motion—No Need for a Potion Spell

My heart is beating and I am alive
Whatever I wish for is bound to thrive.

As you move along repeat this little ditty, and in between, focus your mind on whatever you want to bring into your life. Alternate the rhyme with thoughts that are pertinent to the things you would like to create. This spell is perfect for anyone who is working on improving her shape or losing weight. While you're walking or peddling your butt off, your mind is functioning in full support of the process.

Making Magic in the Snow

I live in a winter vacation spot where everyone comes just to play in the snow. Winter sports aren't my thing, but I spend plenty of time outdoors in the cold, clean air. People think snow is there to ski and slide on, but I found out a long time ago that it's perfect for casting circles too. Since I've been on the go, I've done a lot of spontaneous magic out in the middle of nowhere on days when the rest of the world is indoors by the fire.

The next time you're vacationing in some snowy clime, throw on your warm clothes and go cast a spell. If it happens to be snowing hard, remember that every flake is a crystal. Whatever you focus your mind on will enter these tiny flakes as they fall to the ground and be held there until the snow melts. There's no need to bring along any para-phernalia because the snow takes care of everything for you. Here's how to cast a circle and do magic in the snow.

Once you find a good spot to work in, go to the north and walk around in a circle toward the east. Keep moving around to the south and west until you come to the north point again. It's a good idea to retrace your steps three times, to make sure your circle isn't just a chain of footsteps.

Once that's done go to the north and stomp down the snow to mark the north quarter. Do the same thing at the other three directions. Walk to the north, east, south, and west points and call in each of the Guardians. You will probably be all by yourself, so you can invoke the spirits right out loud if you want to. I always say, "Guardians of the Watchtower of the north (east, west, and south), we invite you to wit-ness this rite and protect this sacred space." But you can say anything you want, whatever your heart calls you to do.

Now go to the north point and, facing south, walk in a straight line across the circle, stopping at the south quarter. Then go to the east and, facing west, walk in a straight line to the west quarter. The space in the middle of the circle where these two lines intersect will be the place where you do your magic from. The center point is where earth and sky connect, and that's where the power of spirit really comes through.

If you happen to have kids or dogs helping you out, set the inten-tion for it to be OK for them to cross over the perimeter of the circle. This applies any time you do magic, by the way. Dogs, cats, and chil-dren are allowed to go in and out of a circle whenever they want to. If you're working alone, stay inside this sacred space and don't leave the circle till your magic is done. You can use the center pathways to get from one point to another.

When everything is set up, go sit right on the center point. Align your body so that your feet are aimed toward the south, and lie down on your back in the snow. Close your eyes and spread your arms out to your sides. Slow your breathing down and listen to the flakes of snow as they fall to the ground. When your mind is still, bring your attention to whatever you wish to manifest and say the following words out loud three times:

Snow Rhyme

Every crystal in the snow
Holds my wish and makes it grow
My inner vision and witch's sight
Will help to bring it to the light.

Once these words are said, make a snow angel. As you move your arms and legs, see your wish going down into the earth and up into the sky. Let all your thoughts mingle with the crystalline structures around you, and feel your wish coming true.

Lie there for as long as you want to. When you feel ready, stand up, walk to the north point and, beginning there, release each of the Guardians, one by one. Close the circle by running clockwise around the circumference in a zigzag pattern, and when you're done, head on home.

Clearing Bad Vibes

Whenever we take a vacation, we wind up staying in a hotel, a motel, a B&B, or *somewhere*. Many of these places are loaded with negative frequencies. The invisible energy lines that flow through these buildings can make it impossible to sleep. They can even make it very difficult to get along or feel at ease. When you only have two weeks off and you're trapped in a room with nothing but bad vibes it can ruin an otherwise good time.

It is very easy to eliminate these interference lines with a couple of dowsing rods. If you take the time to do this, it'll make your vacation much more pleasant. Don't be the least bit concerned about whether you can dowse or not. It's so easy even a child can do it. And if you're a witch, dowsing is one of those things you really ought to have in your bag of tricks.

Before you leave on your trip, go to the hardware store and buy a package of eighteen-inch metal welding rods. Just ask the guy who works there to point you in the right direction. It'll cost less than five bucks. Tuck these in your suitcase. If you happen to be flying, remember that the guards at the security checkpoints aren't fond of sharp, pointed objects, so pack them in your *checked* luggage, *not* in your carry-on. Once you get settled in your room, figure out where north, south, east, and west are.

The first frequencies you'll want to check for will be coming into the room from the south and the west.

Open the package of welding rods and bend two of them into an L-shape. Hold the short end of the rods lightly in your hands and start by walking forward, parallel to the south wall of your hotel room. As you do this, "tell" the rods that you're looking for negative frequencies coming in from the south. If there is negative energy entering the room from that direction, the rods will either open or cross when you get to an energy line. When this happens take one of the unbent rods from the package you bought, place it up against the baseboard right where the line comes in, and leave it there. This causes the frequencies entering the space to arc up and over it, leaving the area you're spending time in free and clear.

Once you've done the south wall, follow the same procedure, walking parallel to the west wall. After you've got the south and west walls cleared, do the same thing on the north and east walls of the room.

If you run out of welding rods, you can block the lines by sliding the flat side of a wire coat hanger up against the baseboard. You can even use coat hangers as dowsing rods by holding the flat side in your hands and letting the movement of the hook indicate where the negative frequencies are.

In the beginning you may be tentative about your ability to do this, but with practice it'll become second nature to you. What I like about using this clearing technique is that it really changes the vibes in the room and makes your time away much more fun. You'll probably notice such a big difference that you'll go home and use this technique to clear your whole house.

I learned about dowsing for and clearing negative frequencies from a guy named Slim Spurling. Slim is a world-class dowser and an amazing man. He has invented the technology to clear up 80 percent of the pollution on the planet. If you want to know more about how to dowse give me a call! And if you're curious about Slim's work, check out his Web site at *www.slimspurling.com.*

Keep in mind that the rhymes and spells in this chapter can be adapted to suit *any* purpose you might have. Be creative with them and remember that they can be used even when you're *not* on vacation. It never hurts to do a Sunrise Spell during the work week, for instance. And you can sit outside under the night sky and do magic on any night of the year if you want to. You don't have to save any of these spells for special occasions. While it may be easier to make time for magic during the two weeks you have off, being an on-the-go witch ultimately comes down to realizing that it's a twenty-four-hour-a-day thing–because you're a witch *all* the time, not just on Sundays and holidays!

Chapter 6

Planes, Trains, and Broomsticks

Planes and trains are a big part of life nowadays. A lot of us on-the-go witches pass through the airport and the train terminal on a regular basis. Some of us are so accustomed to this that getting our bags checked seems as normal as standing in line at the grocery store. This level of "on-the-go-ness" is really no different from going to the mall–except for all the security checks they put you through these days.

Getting dropped off at the terminal is definitely more of a chore now. And getting picked up after a trip isn't what it used to be either. Whoever comes to get you can't wait outside–they have to pay to park the car, come into the terminal, and find you. The safety precautions really block the flow of getting from A to B, and even if you're a witch, there's no way around these external controls. Ironically, they hang *us* up more than they do the average person.

Since most witches carry "questionable" paraphernalia everywhere they go, it's inevitable that Homeland Security will have a bigger problem with what's in *your* bag than they will with everyone else's. The X-ray machine goes haywire scanning the items in a witch's carry-on, never mind her luggage!

I once got detained for half an hour because the officials at the Denver Airport thought the crystal mobile stuffed in my backpack was a secret weapon. When they took it out to inspect it, they discovered my tarot cards too. This held me hostage for another quarter of an hour because they felt compelled to go through the whole deck looking for microfilm.

When that annoying buzzer goes off because the radar can't tell the difference between a pendulum and a switchblade, you turn into a traitor. And every traitor has to take off her shoes so the security guys can make sure there's no bomb in her granny boots. This takes a few extra minutes. Once your shoes are off, they tell you to stand on top of a pair of little footprints so you can get scanned with what looks like a cattle prod. This *always* slows things down. The underwire in your favorite bra or the locket you're wearing *might* be a threat to national security. And these things have to be fully investigated before you can get on with your departure.

If you're going through customs, it's even more of a hassle. Just waiting in line can take hours. And once it's your turn to have your bags inspected, you never know what will happen. If the official rifling through your suitcase decides that the German chocolate you've brought home for the kids has European cooties on it, they'll make you go sit in the corner until they determine whether you're smuggling biochemicals or just being a good mother.

Homeland Security has taken all the fun out of air travel. And riding on the train over any distance is more of a production than it ever was. What was once sort of an exciting thing to do is now fraught with considerations that require extra time and inconvenience. Witches do have to put up with these things, but there are ways to make it all less of a pain if you know what to do.

The spells that follow are for those of you who do a lot of traveling by air or rail.

Planes

We're going to start with a Fear of Flying spell, because even seasoned flyers can be deathly afraid of getting on a plane. And those of us who wouldn't normally be nervous about air travel have become so through media reports suggesting that some guy with a bomb in his briefcase might be sitting in the next seat.

I fly all the time and absolutely love it. Wondering if the plane's going to crash isn't a problem for me. I know my plane won't go down because *I'm* on it! God needs me here to keep doing the work that I do. Those of you who aren't as cocksure about things like this are welcome to use the Fear of Flying Spell and Mojo whenever you travel by air.

Fear of Flying Spell and Mojo

What you will need:

A mortar and pestle
A blue candle
A nail
A stick of Musk incense
A blue pouch
A feather
A tablespoon of celery seeds
A tablespoon of comfrey

A tablespoon of sage
Three drops of Myrrh oil
Your on-the-go spell kit

Because this particular issue is both chronic and predictable, the preparations for it are a bit more elaborate and they need to be made in advance. Part of this spell involves making up a charm bag that you will be able to take with you *anytime* you fly. The herbs and seeds that go into this bag can be found at any good health food store, as can the myrrh oil. Feathers are easy to come by, and you can buy a pouch or make one out of blue satin or velvet. Even cotton will do.

Since this is something that you'll have plenty of time to put together, I would suggest using the light of the full Moon to empower what you're doing. I would also do it in a circle. After all, the fear of flying is a big deal for anyone who suffers from it. And if you want to neutralize it, you might as well give it all you've got.

Gather your ingredients and cast a circle. Call in all four of the Guardians, starting at the north and moving clockwise to the east, south, and west. Anoint your third eye with a drop of myrrh oil, and carve the words "I know I am safe and free of all fear" into the candle with the nail. Etch the Algiz rune ᛉ on the candle too. Algiz is a protection symbol, and it's useful in any situation where you feel vulnerable or afraid.

Now anoint the candle from the wick to the base with myrrh oil. Once that's done, set it in a candleholder and light it. Get the incense going with the candle flame and let the smoke fill up the air.

Place the celery seeds, the comfrey, and the sage into the mortar. Celery seeds have long been used in flying potions, and they make it much easier for a witch to fly. Comfrey is basically a life preserver, and sage is a protection herb. Sage also dispels fear and negativity.

Grind the herbs and seeds with the pestle, keeping your thoughts focused on faith and safety. Put three drops of myrrh oil into the mixture and keep on grinding until you feel that you're done. Myrrh carries protection frequencies, and the oil will serve to bind the herbs and enhance their innate powers.

Now hold the feather in your left hand and charge it with your intentions for safety, freedom from fear, and trust that God is always there, watching over you. When this feels complete, open your on-the-go spell kit and write the following words on one of your Post-it notes:

Fear of Flying Rhyme

My life is always in good hands
God is always there
He'll see that my plane safely lands
Every time I go by air.

Read these words out loud, three times, and dab the paper with three drops of myrrh. Kiss it once to give it life, fold it up, and tuck it safely in the charm bag. Add the feather to the bag, along with the herbs, and sit for a few moments with your eyes closed, quietly feeling in your heart that all of this is true. When you feel ready, send the Guardians home and release the circle.

The bag you've just made can now be taken along with you whenever you have to fly. Carry it in your pocket or purse. Chances are they won't, but if airport security has a problem with it, make up a story. Tell them it's a sachet or a pouch full of herbal tea. Actually, it might be better to tell them the truth, so, if anyone asks, say that you're deathly afraid of flying and this is a good-luck charm.

The next phase of the Fear of Flying Spell is very simple. While you wait for your plane and before you step on board, repeat the Fear of Flying Rhyme at least three times silently, to yourself. Once you're on the plane, and at any time during your flight, if you start to feel nervous, take out your mojo bag and hold it in your right hand. If you want to, you can also repeat the rhyme like a mantra until you calm down.

Trains

The Fear of Flying Spell can be easily adapted if you're one of those people who rides the rails with secret fears of train wrecks. You will follow the same procedure to make your bag. By that I mean, you should take advantage of the full Moon and cast a formal circle. The only difference here is that you will use different paraphernalia and different words. Here are the instructions and ingredients for a railway mojo:

Train Spell and Mojo

What you will need:

A mortar and pestle
A green or brown candle
Myrrh oil
A nail
A green or brown pouch
A tablespoon of dirt
A tablespoon of sea salt
A tablespoon of comfrey
A tablespoon of sage
A stick of patchouli incense
Your on-the-go spell kit

Use the full Moon for this. Gather all your ingredients together and cast a circle. Call in the Guardians, starting at the north and moving clockwise. Carve the words "I am always safe and free of fear" into the candle, along with the Algiz rune ᛉ. Anoint the candle, wick to base, with the myrrh oil and place a dab on your third eye. Light the candle and stick it in a candleholder in front of you. Use the candle flame to light the patchouli incense and let the smoke fill up the air.

Place the dirt, sea salt, and herbs into the mortar, and grind them with intent. Focus your thoughts on safety and freedom from fear. Add three drops of myrrh oil to bind the herbs, and keep grinding till you feel finished.

Open your on-the-go spell kit and write the following words on a Post-it note:

Train Rhyme

Locomotive, choo-choo train,
Carry me safe and sound
Every fear goes down the drain
God goes wherever I'm bound.

Read this rhyme out loud three times and anoint the paper with three drops of myrrh. Draw the Algiz rune ᛉ over it with your forefinger, kiss the paper, fold it up, and place it in your pouch. Pour the mixture from the mortar into the charm bag. Hold the pouch in your left hand and charge it with safe thoughts. When you feel ready, send the Guardians home and release the circle.

This charm bag can now be carried in your pocket or purse whenever you travel by rail. Be sure to repeat the above rhyme before you get on board, and feel free to repeat it quietly to yourself at any time during your journey.

Boats

If traveling by water makes you nervous, adapt the instructions above and follow the same directions, using the ingredients and the words listed below.

Water Charm

What you will need:

A mortar and pestle
A sea-green or blue pouch
A sea-green or blue candle
A nail
Myrrh oil
A piece or some shavings of Ivory soap
Three LifeSavers candies
A cork
Your on-the-go spell kit

After you cast your circle, place the last three ingredients in the mortar and grind them with three drops of myrrh oil. When you're done mixing everything together, take some Post-it notes and write down the following rhyme. Read it aloud three times, anoint it with three drops of myrrh, kiss it, and add it to the pouch, along with the mortar and pestle mixture.

Water Rhyme

Floating on the briny deep
This charm bag next to me I keep
I jinxed all fear with my mortar and pestle
Nothing can sink this sturdy vessel.

Take this charm bag with you whenever you travel by water. If your fears get the best of you during your voyage, hold the pouch in your right hand and repeat the above rhyme like a mantra until you calm down.

Keep Moving

Now that our fears are out of the way, let's move on! Any witch who's catching planes and trains on a regular basis is too busy to afford the time it takes to get held up by security officials, missed flights, lost luggage, or late trains. When you commute by rail or have to catch a shuttle, any type of logistical snafu can make you miss important meetings, appointments, and interviews. Sometimes there just isn't enough time to make a plane connection, and it's stressful to wonder if it's humanly possible to make it from one end of O'Hare to another in five minutes. (Take my word for it, it's impossible–but I've done it.)

I travel by air mostly. To iron out every possible kink that might come up during the "Magical Mystery Tour" through the terminal, I use the following spell. It's an all- purpose sort of charm that covers every problem. You can use it whenever and wherever you want to make sure that *nothing* holds you up.

No Problemo Spell

What you will need:

Your on-the-go spell kit
A bottle of spring water

This spell is so simple you can do it on your way to the terminal. It will clear away anything that might jinx your trip. To begin with, cast an energetic circle around your body, about six feet in diameter. Imagine that this invisible circle of protection moves with you as you move, like a hoop skirt. Invite each of the Guardians in and ask them to stick around for the duration of the trip, just to make sure nothing goes wrong.

Open your on-the-go spell kit and anoint your third eye with a drop of musk oil. Holding the quartz crystal up to your third eye, program it for a smooth and hassle-free travel experience, using the following rhyme:

No Problemo Rhyme

As I go to catch my plane (train)
All problems will be jinxed
This crystal will serve to keep things sane
And smooth out all the kinks.

Tuck the crystal in your pocket, or stick it in your bra near your heart. Once it's safely hidden away, take out the bottle of spring water and drink every drop. As you do this, envision any problem that might arise being flushed away.

When all of this is done, your energy field will be completely clear, and nothing will get in your way. Keep your energetic circle active until after you've picked up your baggage and have arrived safely at your final destination point.

Dagaz and Algiz

For those of you who are too "on the go" to be bothered with spells and rhymes, there's an even simpler way to make sure there aren't any logistical glitches to snarl up your traveling experience. All you have to do is draw or paint a bind rune on your luggage, your carry-on, and the palm of the hand you write with. A bind rune is a combination of two or more runes that unites the magical properties of each one in the form of a symbol or talisman.

Since the main goal in this particular type of situation is to protect yourself from problems and be immune to overzealous scrutiny, you'll be using the Dagaz rune and the Algiz rune ᛞ ᛉ.

We've mentioned Dagaz a few times already. The reason I like to use it at the airport is that it makes you invisible to that one security screener who is just *looking* for someone to hassle. Most of them are just doing their job, but you know the one I mean!

I like to bind Dagaz with the Algiz rune. Algiz protects you from everything. When you're en route to anywhere, it insulates you from having to worry about anything going wrong. It forms a kind of "energetic umbrella" that deflects all the petty, uncontrollable interference that everyone runs into when they travel.

If you travel regularly, or are just too busy for spells and rhymes, you can apply the Dagaz-Algiz bind rune *permanently* to your baggage and carry-on luggage. That way it'll always be there and you won't have to think about it before every trip. The best way to do this is to go to the craft store, pick out your favorite color of liquid paint, and draw the image shown above, somewhere on your suitcases.

As far as your purse goes, you can take the tube of liquid paint and draw the same image on one of the inside flaps of your pocketbook. It won't show and there's really nothing wrong with having this type of protection around *wherever* you go. I always draw this bind rune on my hand too. You can use a ballpoint pen or just do an energetic drawing and trace the rune over your palm with your forefinger. Either way is OK.

Fellow Travelers

When you're on the go, the hours you spend in the air or rolling across the countryside in a train belong to you and you alone. No one can expect anything from you when you're moving between point A and point B. I look forward to long flights because I know I can *use* that time to write, study, or meditate.

The problem is, *you never know whom you will be sitting next to.* And if your traveling companions have babies, are talkative, or drink like a fish, it interferes with your plans in a big way. I have a special spell that I use to circumvent the possibility of being plopped down next to someone whose issues might interfere with what I want to do. If you're someone who needs to make the most of the time you spend commuting or traveling, the following spell will come in handy.

Peace and Quiet Spell

What you will need:

Your on-the-go spell kit

The best time to do this is right before you board the train, or while you sit waiting at the airport departure gate. If you haven't already done so, cast an energetic circle and call in the Guardians. Close your eyes for a few minutes and bring yourself back to center. Open your eyes, get out your spell kit, and anoint your third eye with a drop of musk oil. Take out a Post-it note and draw the following three pictures on it: a pair of lips, a baby bottle or a breast, and a picture of a martini glass. Enclose these images inside a circle and draw an X over the whole thing.

On a second Post-it note, write down the following rhyme:

Serenity Now Rhyme

Whenever I travel here and there
Noise and disturbance aren't part of the fare
People just seem to let me be
Peace and quiet ride with me.

If you can say these words out loud without drawing attention to yourself, do it. Don't worry about it if you can't, but either way, dab three drops of musk oil on the paper, hold it to your lips for a moment, and fold it up. Tuck it away in your pocket, or stuff it safely in your bra, near your heart.

It will delight you to find, upon taking your seat, that your fellow travelers have no interest in talking, no children, and no passion for alcohol. Most of the time I find that whoever sits next to me wants to sleep or read the trip away, and this leaves me free to do whatever I please.

There was only one time this spell *didn't* work for me. I was flying back from Denver to Burlington, and on the way to the departure gate I passed a very hip-looking "witchy woman" on the escalator. The two of us recognized each other immediately, as witches are prone to do.

I had big plans to get some work done, and I cracked up laughing when I got on the plane and fate seated me next to her. It turned out that she was an astrologer too and, aside from having a million other things in common, we were both Virgos with the Moon in Aries. I felt as if she was my long-lost sister. We talked the whole way home, and learned a lot from each other.

I'm relating this story because the "best laid plans of mice and men" are often not what your spirit needs at the time. So, do this spell to preserve your peace and serenity, but be open to the fact that serendipity is always a factor and plays a big role in what you learn about yourself while you're on the go.

Buses and Subways

A lot of on-the-go witches live in the city and have to use public transportation all the time. I haven't had to take a bus or travel by subway in over thirty years, so it's hard for me to remember what this is like. As I recall, there are two main problems when you commute this way—finding a seat and getting stuck sitting next to a lunatic.

Back in chapter 3, we talked about how easy it is to visualize a parking space. You can use the same technique to create a seat on the bus or the subway. All you have to do is picture the perfect seat in your mind's eye as clearly as possible while you're waiting for the next bus or train to roll up. It's not that complicated, and you don't have to go through a lot of rigmarole.

If you don't trust your powers of manifestation, the following charm will not only guarantee you a good seat, it will also ensure that you don't end up sitting next to a serial killer. Repeat this rhyme silently to yourself while you wait for the bus or while you're standing on the subway platform.

Safe and In Good Company Charm

The perfect seat is always found
I never have to stand
And lunatics don't come around
Because they've made other plans.

If you're going to use this charm, keep a copy of it in your wallet until you memorize it. It's really OK to make up your own charm right on the spot–don't feel restricted by my way of doing things, and don't feel that it won't work if you don't come up with a good rhyme. It's the *intention* that matters, not the poetry.

I hope that the information in this chapter makes your life easier. If you use what I've shared with you here, you'll find that traveling back and forth over short or long distances becomes less of a routine and more of an adventure. Knowing enough to take your broomstick along wherever you go makes getting from A to B a lot more fun.

Chapter 7

Winding Down the Witch

There's a lot to be said for being on the go. Having a full and rewarding life is a rare and precious gift, and it implies that some part of you lives with a sense of purpose–or knows that you came here to make a difference. When you realize how lucky you are to be this blessed, something in you strives to meet a higher standard and you tend to work harder. Why this is, I'm not quite sure, but I do know that it can get you into trouble.

There's something dangerously addictive about loving life and loving what you do. And while being passionately involved has its good points, it's easy to cross the line that turns you from a human *being* into a human *doing*, and lose touch with the still point in the center that keeps everything balanced.

I am an expert at lecturing others on the virtues of taking time to smell the roses, but I rarely practice what I preach. I must confess that the side effects of being unable to heed my own advice have caught up with me more than once. Parts of this book were written while I was feeling sick as a dog, all because I thought I could treat myself like a machine.

You'd think we'd know when to slow down, but very few of us have that kind of wisdom. The part of us that wants to act as if we're superhuman is very good at pulling the wool over our eyes. It may be an exercise in futility to include this chapter, but I'm going to do it anyway just because there's an outside chance that you *might* open to this page on a day when the Bionic Mistress in your brain needs to be put in her place.

There are many different ways to stop driving yourself up the wall or into the ground. When you start to notice that your wonderful life is getting to be too much, use the following technique to help you understand what to do about it.

Am I Crazy, or Is This Too Much?

Give yourself at least fifteen minutes alone to do this. Sit quietly in a chair and close your eyes. Slow your breathing down and tell your thoughts they can take over again in a little while. When you feel centered and ready, say the following rhyme out loud.

Is It Me?

Is this real or is it fake?
Do I see what's true?
It seems that it's time to take a break,
But there's way too much to do.
Should I go or should I stop?
Tell me now before I pop!

Once these words are spoken, remain still with your eyes closed and listen to the voice that comes from inside. The inner answer is *always* immediate and it *always* speaks the truth. Trust what you're told and use that information to help you decide how to proceed from there. Most of the time the messages I receive when I do this are quite simple. I hear things like "You need more rest (more water, more love, etc.)." "Just play" is something that I hear a lot.

Every now and then the messages aren't so simple, so be prepared for anything. You may get very explicit instructions that you're not quite ready to follow. If your inner voice tells you to quit your job, you don't necessarily have to follow through–but you may find that in the long run this is what you end up doing.

Pendulums

If you have reservations about trusting your "inner voice," you can always use a pendulum to ask yourself if it's time to take a breather. Good pendulums can be found at any metaphysical shop, or you can make one out of a paper clip and a piece of string. Lockets and necklaces can double as pendulums too.

Holding the pendulum in your dominant hand, say the following rhyme:

"Yes" or "No" Rhyme

Up and down,
Nods "Yes,"
Back and forth
Says "No."

*Let me know if it's time
To relax and go with the flow.*

If you've gotten to the point where you actually *need* to take out a pendulum and do this, chances are your answer is going to be "Yes." If it is, the question is: What do you do next?

Stopping the madness doesn't always require extreme measures. If your on-the-go hamster wheel has broken its axle, a week off *may* be the only solution–but it doesn't have to come down to that. What I do when I reach the breaking point is ask myself, "What would make me happy right now? What would I love to do more than anything?"

I'm not a really complicated person, and it doesn't bother me to confess that I head to the thrift shop when I'm overwhelmed. The two or three hours this involves gets me away from my work and always yields wonderful surprises. Call me crazy, but picking up a pair of Armani jeans and a couple of designer outfits for under five bucks makes me feel as if I've pulled off a major coup. It's a simple, nowhere thing to do, but it never fails to make me happy.

What works for you will be different from what works for me, but the point here is that this business of taking the pressure off doesn't have to be a big deal. And if you can pay enough attention to your needs, so that you know when you should get away for a few hours, you'll save yourself a heap of trouble.

The truth is, most of the time all we need is a nap, an afternoon to ourselves, or a bath. Since a bath is such a terrific way to sort things out, and something you can do *anytime* you feel like it, here's an all-purpose bath spell that will send every ounce of tension right down the drain.

Magical Bath

What you will need:

A cup of sea salt
A cup of Epsom salts
Three drops of lavender oil
Three bags of chamomile tea
Sage or frankincense incense
A white candle

Shut off the phone and lock the doors. As the tub fills up with water, anoint the candle from the base to the wick with lavender oil. Light it and use the flame to get your incense going. Pour the sea salt and the Epsom salts into the tub and stir them in well. Add the lavender oil and the chamomile tea bags. Mix everything together and, when the tub is full, hop in and start to soak.

You won't have to worry too much about consciously releasing anything, because the Epsom-sea salt combination has a way of pulling it right out of you. Floating in the water, feel yourself stripped of all care. Know that this cleansing process is a sacred act that will bring you back to a place of wholeness.

Stay in the water for as long as you want to. If at some point during your bath you feel called to offer up a prayer, do so in your own words, or feel free to use the following rhyme:

The "I Surrender" Rhyme

As I bathe my heart in the waters of life
The cares that fill it dissolve

There's no need for worry and no trace of strife
Every problem just seems to resolve.
With each breath come feelings of peace
I remember now why I am here
My trust in myself will never cease
I surrender all of my fear.

When you feel completely relaxed and ready to move on to what's next, pull out the plug, get out of the tub, and dry off. Anoint your skin with lotion and wrap yourself up in a soft clean robe. Don't talk or think about doing anything for now. Go crawl into bed and sleep for a while. When you awaken you will feel rejuvenated and refreshed. Start your day over again with a strong cup of good coffee or a hot cup of tea, and give yourself half an hour of privacy to reflect on what your real needs are.

Just so you know—this bathing ritual is one of those sure bets. Don't hesitate to use it whenever you need to.

One Hour a Day, All to Yourself

Another way I maintain my sanity in the midst of a busy life is to give myself one hour every day to do *only* what I please. During this time I stop what I'm doing and put my attention on what I want to do instead of what I have to do. Sometimes I nap. Sometimes I click on the TV and watch cowboy movies. Sometimes I flop down on the couch with a couple of cookies and a copy of *The National Enquirer*. It's different every day. And when the sixty minutes are up, I go right back to work.

The point of giving yourself this hour is to let the *adult you* off her leash and tune in to the part of you that doesn't need to be grown-up and responsible. It's like having a window in the day that you can climb out of—or like what recess used to be, minus all the jerks on the playground! And no matter how much you have to tend to throughout the rest of the day, you always know that you will have a *choice* about what goes on during this one-hour period. It's a way of showing yourself that life doesn't have to be *only* about accomplishing things. Sometimes doing nothing in particular is the most productive way to use your time.

A witch needs to maintain a close connection to her inner self on a daily basis. It's probably the most important part of the "job." You can't expect your spells to work, and you can't remain tuned in to the rhythms of the natural world if you're distracted, anxious, and out of touch. If you become too scattered in outer things and lose the directions to that place within, your creative abilities and your magical abilities will yield mediocre results at best.

A real witch knows how important it is to go into her heart every day. Doing this makes all of her outer activities more focused, whether they are everyday things or magical things. The peaceful center in the eye of the storm is free of all disturbance. When you live your life from that place, the hurricane swirling around you is much easier to handle.

There are many paths to the center, so take your pick. Just remember to go there. Make it your mission to deepen your connection to your own spirit. A ritual bath, an hour alone, a long walk in the forest, silent prayers, sacred movement, or deep meditation—any or all of these things can take you home to the peaceful quietness inside your heart.

Exercise, etc.

Anyone will tell you that exercise is a good way to unwind, and I think it works for some people. If it works for you, by all means keep doing it.

The only thing you have to watch out for is that exercise can become just another form of regimentation.

Fitting in your workout, your yoga class, your walk, your tai chi instructions, or *whatever* can end up being counterproductive if you're not careful. Exercise takes effort and discipline and is a control-based activity—so if you're going to do it, just make sure you pay attention to how it really makes you feel. As long as you *love* it, you have my permission to keep it up.

For those of you who are too on-the-go to work out, I suggest that you look into the possibility of purchasing a device known as a Chi Machine. A Chi Machine is a wonderful tool that has positive health benefits and psychological benefits as well. It's just a little motorized box that you lie down and rest your ankles on.

When you turn it on, the ankle rests move back and forth, and this action oscillates your spine in a beneficial way. Ten minutes on a Chi Machine is equivalent to a thirty-minute walk, girls! I use mine *all* the time. It appears to keep my weight and my blood pressure down. It also cures my headaches and counteracts my bouts with insomnia. Any seriously on-the-go witch *needs* a Chi Machine in her life!

Meditation

There are so many erroneous, preconceived notions about witches and witchery. Thanks to the Inquisition, most people see us as deviates, hysterics, or wanton outcasts who have lost control of themselves completely. The truth is, witches are more grounded and more in touch with what's real about life than they're given credit for. As we continue to come out of the closet it will be easier for others to recognize that there's nothing strange or scary about us at all. We just happen to have *remarkable abilities.*

Some witches are born with these abilities. These are the gals who come from a long line of witches–their abilities are inherited. Others, like myself, have had previous lives as witches but no trace of witchery in the family tree this time around. Many come to the magical arts for no apparent reason at all except for the fact that they are intuitively drawn to express themselves in this way.

People think that psychic powers and divinatory skills are "just there" in every witch. This is true for some, but not for all. Regardless of whether these remarkable abilities come with the package or have to be developed, the only way for any witch to keep her skills in alignment with the forces of light is by maintaining her connection to spirit.

Laurie Cabot, the famous "Witch of Salem" teaches her students that *light carries information*. When you allow yourself an hour of meditation each day your body, mind, and spirit, are *infused* with spiritual light for that length of time. As you bring more light in, the information you receive from it fills you with higher knowledge, a deeper kind of wisdom, and extraordinary abilities.

I found out a long time ago that no one can teach you how to be psychic, how to read cards, or how to do magic. These things are learned only through the gradual development of the sixth sense. My own experience with meditation has shown me that my sixth sense grows more powerful *only* through the act of going within. As I become more familiar with this part of my nature, my psychic powers and other remarkable abilities increase.

These special powers come with an obligation to maintain a high level of integrity when it comes to how you use them. Regardless of how you find your way to witchcraft, your spells won't work and your sixth sense won't develop if you don't keep your focus on matters of spirit. With that in mind, let's talk about meditation.

Never having been well heeled enough afford regular therapy, I would have lost it a long time ago if I didn't know about meditation. It has saved my life. Contrary to popular belief, you don't need a guru to teach you how. Anyone can meditate. The problem is, people get discouraged when they try it. If they don't see the Universal Deity right away, they assume they're doing it wrong and just give up on the idea.

I teach meditation, and it amazes me that people try it a few times and decide to stop because they think they don't have what it takes. It would make as much sense to strap on a pair of skis and expect to win Olympic gold on the first try. I find it a very interesting reflection on the enormity of the average human ego that *anyone* would think they could knock on heaven's door once and expect the Supreme Being to come racing down the stairs to see what they want. *I mean, come on!*

Meditation is like everything else in life–the more you practice, the more you learn about it. After a while it becomes an important part of your day, and you wouldn't dream of skipping it any more than you would think about leaving the house in the morning without brushing your teeth. I have reached the point where I no longer question the need to "go to the well," and I do it with reverence and humility.

There are a million different ways to meditate and get centered. I am going to share a couple of simple techniques that I use on a daily basis. The first one is known as "The Unity Breath."

Instructions for the Unity Breath

Give yourself at least half an hour to do this. If you think you will be disturbed, unplug the phone, lock the door, and tell whoever's around to leave you alone for a while.

Sitting quietly in a chair or on the floor, close your eyes and slow your breathing down. Let all your thoughts find their place in line and tell them to pipe down! Listen to your breath and feel it going in and out. Let the sound of your heart beating reach your ears, and become as still as you can.

Centered in your heart, imagine that there is a tube running through your body, parallel to your spine, from the center of the top of your head down to the opening between your legs. Imagine that every time you breathe, the life force from the greater universe enters this tube from both ends, flows into your heart, and keeps recirculating–so that what comes in gets sent out to the universe with each exhale, and returns with every inhale, as if circulated by a pump.

Keep this image of the tube clear in your mind and continue breathing in the life force as you bring your attention to the base of your spine. Visualize a cord extending out from the base of your spinal column, and see it going down through the floor, all the way to the center of the Earth. Watch this cord as it penetrates every layer of soil and rock, and see it as it finally reaches the inner core of the planet. Tie it there in an imaginary knot. Give it a little tug if you want to, to make sure the connection is secure.

Now bring your consciousness back up to your heart. From within your heart, *feel* the love that you have inside for Mother Earth. Remind yourself that you are her own precious child–everything you are and everything you have comes from her. She has watched over you through each and every one of your lifetimes. Think of the beauty of nature, if it helps to stir your feelings. Call up as much emotion as you can.

When all the love that you have in your heart for Mother Earth reaches its fullest capacity, form it into a golden ball and send it down into her core. Let that love touch the heart of the Great Mother–let her *feel* how much you love her.

Continue breathing and, as you do, feel all the love that Mother Earth has for you, coming back up through the cord you created and filling your heart. It may take a few minutes, but you will feel this. She has loved you unconditionally from the beginning, and she will love you that way forever, no matter what.

With your heart full of love from the Great Mother, turn your attention now to Father Sky. In the same way that you sent a cord down into the heart of the Earth, you are now going to visualize a cord going out of the top of your head all the way into the deepest reaches of space. When this cord reaches the heart of the Father aspect of creation, tie it there and make the connection secure.

Now go back into your heart and call up all the feelings you have for your Father aspect. The Father aspect is the part of creation that isn't directly related to the earthly realm. The infinite vastness of the sky–the sun, the Moon, the planets, and the stars–the lightning and the thunder–these things are all ruled by "Father" energy.

Imagine all the angelic beings who have watched over your spirit since it was created, and see if it helps you connect with the deep love you have for your Father aspect. When you feel ready, form this love into a golden ball and send it up the cord you created, all the way into the deepest reaches of space. Allow the Great Spirit to *feel* your love for him.

Continue breathing and, as you do, let all the infinite love your Father has for you come down through this cord and fill up your heart. It may take a minute or two, but you will feel this, or sense it, or know it somehow. Let the love from your Father merge with the love from your Mother inside your heart space, and know that when these two forces come together inside you, you can begin to see and know the oneness of the Father/Mother/Child God within.

Remain centered here within and continue meditating for as long as you wish to. When you feel ready, open your eyes and go about your business.

The Heart Meditation

On days when you have time, you can go a little deeper if you want to. I like to go directly from the Unity Breath into what's known as the Heart Meditation. This meditation is an extremely powerful healing technique and a very simple and direct way to connect with the Light within you.

The instructions for the Heart Meditation were included in my second book, *The Old Girls' Book of Dreams*, so some of you may already know about this process. It's also written about and fully explained by the man who taught it to me, Drunvalo Melchizedek, in a book called *Living in the Heart*. If you're interested in learning about the sacred space within the heart, I recommend that you read Drunvalo's book.

For those of you who have never heard of the Heart Meditation, I am going to include the instructions for it here so you can use it whenever you want to.

Instructions for the Heart Meditation

Once you've completed all the steps for the Unity Breath, remain where you are and continue breathing. Before you move on to the Heart Meditation it's a good idea to put on a blindfold or cover your eyes with a scarf. Something about the total absence of light makes it easier to do this process, so have some sort of blindfold ready, or just put one on before you start the Unity Breath, so you don't have to think about it.

To begin with, bring your awareness to your head. Now, use your imagination and take your head off. Place it somewhere above or behind you, just for the length of time you are in your heart. There's a reason for this. Your mind and your mental processes don't help when you want to be in the heart space, so it's easier to symbolically detach your head before you start. Don't worry. You'll reattach your head when the meditation is over.

With your head out of the picture, bring your consciousness to the opening at the top of your neck. Feel your awareness inside your throat. Spend a minute or two sensing the inside of your throat and neck. When you feel ready to move on, send your awareness down your esophagus, down past your sternum, and over toward your heart area.

Place your consciousness in front of your heart and imagine it there before you–get a sense of it as a *physical* organ. Don't worry about whether you're doing this correctly, and trust the imagery that you see in your inner vision. There is no wrong way to do this process, and it is *not* a logical affair.

As you picture your heart beating inside you, you're going to have to decide how to enter it. There are two ways to do this. One way is to just allow your consciousness to slip right in through the wall of the heart. This is what's known as "The Female Way."

The second way to enter your heart is "The Male Way." If you choose the male way, you need to know that there is a donut-shaped field of light around the human heart that has an opening in the center. Standing, facing your heart, get a sense of this energy field. See it as it circulates around the organ itself, and notice how it enters the heart from both the top and the bottom. Move your awareness to the opening in this field at the top of your heart and, looking down into it, notice which way it rotates. When you feel ready, relax completely and allow your consciousness to get pulled into this vortex. As you do this, your entire being will be pulled into what's known as your heart chamber.

Regardless of which method you choose to enter your heart, once you get inside, it will probably be very dark. If it is, all you have to do is ask for the light to come. It may come on very suddenly, or it may take a little time, but when the light comes you will find yourself in a chamber of some kind. Notice where you are. This space will be different for each of you.

The Heart Chamber is the place where your soul goes between each and every one of your lifetimes. All the records relating to your purpose for coming to Earth are stored here. The answers to all of your questions can be found here too. The Heart Chamber is like a nerve center that connects you to everything in creation. From this place you can go anywhere and you can do anything.

I like to go into my heart every day. Lately I have been working on living from my heart as much as possible. I use the time I spend there to heal myself, ask questions, or resolve things. Very often I'll invite other people to come in. Miraculous things happen in this place, and I find that just knowing how to do this process has made it much easier to live my life and understand why I am here.

If these instructions seem complicated, don't let that get in the way. With practice you'll find that going into your heart is really quite simple and well worth the time it takes.

OK, So You Don't Have Time

Regardless of how easy it is for me to meditate regularly, I am a realist when it comes to these things. I know that there are always going to be people out there who really believe that they don't have time to fit it in. If that's the way it is in your world, don't feel bad–because there are ways to get around even this.

Since it's not the act of meditating but the *state* it puts you in that keeps you balanced, I'm going to offer those of you who are over the top with your "on-the-go-ness" a meditation replacement that requires no time or effort.

When I don't have time or I'm too messed up to meditate, I use a labyrinth. This may be news to some of you, but if you walk into the center of a labyrinth, stop for a few moments, turn around and walk back out, it generates a feeling of peace and wholeness. You don't have to intend anything or be in an altered state. Just the act of making the turns in succession centers you and brings the left and the right portions of the brain into balance.

What's even better news is that this centering process takes place whether you walk through a big outdoor labyrinth or use a small, hand-held, finger labyrinth. That's right, my friend! Back in the old days, finger labyrinths were carved in stone at the entryways of all the big cathedrals. People would trace their fingers over these carvings before entering the church, as an act of spiritual preparation. Each parishioner would use the finger labyrinth to get centered and whole prior to every mass.

If this method appeals to you, I'm going to suggest a couple of things. If you want to, you can buy a finger labyrinth at any good metaphysical shop. They are also very easy to draw, and I have included a diagram of a seven-circuit labyrinth on the next page for you to use or copy as you wish. Keep your finger labyrinth handy so you can pull it out and use it whenever you need to.

For those of you who are creative, I would suggest painting a large version of the labyrinth on any floor in your house. If this feels too permanent to you, you can make a floor cloth with a painting of a labyrinth on it and use it like a rug or just roll it out when you want to use it. Have fun with this. I've tried it, and it works.

Sometimes It's Really Quite Simple

The problem with having a full and interesting life is that the efforts you put into maintaining a good inner and outer balance can become too studied or contrived. I've watched myself become oh-so-fragile and delicate at times, like some sort of spiritual prima donna, too busy drawing boundaries and creating sacred space to remember that, after all, I'm just a human being here and life is really very simple. There's nothing worse than a witch who takes herself and her sense of purpose too seriously. This, more than most things, makes me want to barf!

In closing, what I would like to do is remind you that even *big girls* just wanna have fun, after all. While I truly do feel that meditation, spiritual bathing rituals, and taking time out are all wonderful things to do, sometimes winding down is just a simple matter of kicking your shoes off and getting real, either by yourself or with someone who wants to get real with you. If you don't take time to do this, it's inevitable that you will turn into an overly serious, self-righteous bore that nobody wants to be around.

The virtues of being true to yourself and of being able to honestly appreciate the value of your own craziness were first brought to my attention when I was sixteen. My father took me to see a little play called *The Madwoman of Chaillot*, and the main character, the Countess Aurelia, made an indelible impression on me. In retrospect you could almost say that I've patterned my life after hers.

What I loved most about the Madwoman was that she wasn't just some rich old bag who hung around being waited on hand and foot—she had a sense of purpose. And in this little play by Jean Giraudoux, this crazy old countess and her two crazy friends devised a plan to lure all the tyrants of the world to their doom.

As serious as she was about the importance of her mission, the Madwoman of Chaillot was far too crazy to take *herself* seriously. And she balanced her life with the regular sipping of a heavenly substance known as Green Chartreuse.

I keep a bottle of Green Chartreuse around in honor of my favorite heroine. And I pour myself a shot whenever the Madwoman in me has had it with the ongoing battle to keep the dark forces in their place. The nice thing about this liqueur is that it's made from the roots of the Angelica plant. Angelica is widely known to draw *angelic forces* into your life. And so aside from giving you a little buzz, the regular sipping of Green Chartreuse will also bring the angelic beings who follow you around in a little closer.

Any witch who's on the go knows that you can't travel faster than your angels can fly—and if your *angels* are willing to interrupt their flight just to join you for a few pops, there must be something pretty special about this green elixir. Chartreuse is potent, so take it in small doses. If you have alcohol issues, or are using any medication that doesn't get along with alcohol, stay away from it completely. But every now and then, when you find yourself taking yourself and your life too seriously, or when the tyrants of the world appear to have the upper hand, let the Madwoman in you come out and try a shot of Green Chartreuse, straight up or on the rocks. It's one of the best ways I've found to get real and hang out with my angels at the same time.

To be a really *great* witch you need to maintain a delicate balance between your *magical* self and the part of you that has to function on the everyday level. In order for your remarkable abilities to shine, you have to know how to walk in two worlds simultaneously.

So many "wanna-be" witches are overly involved with the *mystique* that surrounds the Craft. They get lost in the otherworldly element that unfortunately has followed the Wiccan traditions around, along with a lot of other nonsense, since the Inquisitors twisted the Old Ways into something they were not. People who use their interest in witchcraft and its trappings to set themselves *apart* from others, or as a means to escape into a world of their own, are deluded—about themselves, about life, and about the essence of good magic. This isn't what being a witch is about.

Really great witches have their feet on the ground and are deeply connected to earthly things. They are overjoyed to be living in the real world and happy to have the opportunity to use their abilities for the benefit of all. They know there's nothing hocus-pocus about witchcraft and they don't put on airs. For them magic is simply a means to bring their special powers to bear on the things they wish to change at the physical level. At rock bottom, a witch's abilities are just part of being human.

If you're on the go, the path where the "other" world meets the "real" world is the one you want to be on. You don't have to sacrifice your need for sacredness just because you happen to have a full and interesting outer life. The two can live together happily when you understand that magic isn't separate from the other things you do; it's everywhere, all the time, wherever *you* happen to be.

Appendix

Calling in the Guardians

Here is what I do when I am out and about and want to call in the Guardians. You can follow this method or make up your own way to do it.

In my mind I go to the North point and either whisper or think to myself:

Guardians of the Watchtower of the North, element of Earth, and all of thee in the realm of the Bear. I invite you to witness this rite and protect this sacred space.

When this is done I bring my mind to the East, South, and West points respectively and quietly say the following words at each direction:

Guardians of the Watchtower of the East, element of Air, and all of thee in the realm of the Raven. I invite you to witness this rite and protect this sacred space.

Guardians of the Watchtower of the South, element of Fire, and all of thee in the realm of the Dragon. I invite you to witness this rite and protect this sacred space.

Guardians of the Watchtower of the West, element of Water, and all of thee in the realm of the Mermaid. I invite you to witness this rite and protect this sacred space.

Once you've invoked the Guardians you can go ahead with your spell casting. Just remember to send each one of them back from whence they came when you're done. Anything that's powerful enough to invoke, can't be left twiddling its thumbs at the airport or by the road-side! When it's time to send the Guardians home, this is what I say:

Spirits be gone, return to thy place. Leave peace to reign in time and space.

About the Author

A New England native, Cal Garrison's interest in Magic and the Occult began when she was sixteen. She majored in painting at the Massachusetts College of Art and received her diploma in 1971. Breaking every rule, Cal wrote her senior thesis on astrology. By that time she had renounced art, making the decision to focus solely on matters of spirit.

In 1973, following a two-year apprenticeship with Charles Jayne, Cal began her own astrological practice. Since that time she has done over 3,000 horoscopes and continues to work in this field. Her articles on the subject appear in numerous publications.

Witchcraft, along with her knowledge of herbs and herbal medicine have been part of the picture since day one. These interests run parallel to her search for inner truth. A student of life, and many different spiritual disciplines, Cal found her way to Drunvalo Melchizedek and the Flower of Life Teachings in 1997. A certified Flower of Life Facilitator, she now teaches meditation workshops all over the country.

Through her interest in the Flower of Life, Cal got connected to a man named Slim Spurling. Slim has developed the technology to clear up 80% of the pollution on the planet. Cal works directly with him, doing research in the field of subtle energy. They have co-written a book documenting all of Slim's research. It is titled, *Slim Spurling's Universe–Ancient Science Rediscovered to Restore the Health of the Environment and Mankind.*

Cal's three other books, *The Old Girls' Book of Spells*, *The Old Girls' Book of Dreams*, and *Witch on the Go* address the real aspects of witchcraft in a no-nonsense, down-to-earth way. At the moment she is writing two new books.

The mother of three grown daughters, a West Highland-White terrier by the name of Oliver, and her cat, She-Ra, Cal is living her dream, happily, in the Green Mountains of Vermont.

To Our Readers

Red Wheel, an imprint of Red Wheel/Weiser, publishes books on topics ranging from spunky self-help, spirituality, personal growth, and relationships to women's issues and social issues. Our mission is to publish quality books that will make a difference in people's lives—how we feel about ourselves and how we relate to one another and to the world at large. We value integrity, compassion, and receptivity, both in the books we publish and in the way we do business.

Our readers are our most important resource, and we value your input, suggestions, and ideas about what you would like to see published. Please feel free to contact us, to request our latest book catalog, or to be added to our mailing list.

Red Wheel/Weiser, LLC
P.O. Box 612
York Beach, ME 03910-0612
www.redwheelweiser.com